9780361017831
AF378590

Photos by Pembroke Stephens, Western Mail,
Coloursport, Syndication International,
Colin Elsey and H. W. Neale.
North Wales Weekly News,
Jean Lomas, K. M. Forward.
Cartoons by Richard, Clew and Royle.

Front endpaper
Keith Fielding's try for England & Wales v Scotland & Ireland at Twickenham, part of the 1970–71 Centenary celebrations

Back endpaper
Gareth Edwards scores a spectacular try for Wales v The President's XV in the 1970–71 Centenary Match at Cardiff Arms Park

The World of Rugby

SBN 361 01765 0
Published in 1971 by Purnell, London
© 1971 B.P.C. Publishing Limited
Made and printed in Italy

The World of Rugby
1971-1972

Edited by Jack Cox

PURNELL

London

Contents

The Art of Good
Scrummaging
by Ray Williams

Northampton's lock Lacey up-ended in a poor scrummaging move v Blackheath

A sound scrummaging side is rarely, if ever, outplayed. This expert coaching advice will help any club to achieve better technique.

The most exciting kind of Rugby Union Football is that where there is an abundance of running and handling. Many coaches and players feel that all that is required is for them to practise this aspect of the game and exhilarating rugby will follow as a natural consequence. This is far from the truth for the game can only be played successfully in this way by creating the right platform.

The scrum is the most important single platform in the game. It makes such physical demands that it affects one's ability in the lines-out, in the rucks and mauls, in supporting attacks and in covering in defence. Consequently poor scrummaging affects team performance, whereas a good scrummaging side will rarely be completely out-played in spite of other inadequacies in the team. What then are the essentials of good scrummaging?

Attitude, as in all other facets of the game, looms large! Players must believe that good scrummaging is important. They must be prepared to scrummage for the whole of the game. Many packs begin a game with a rush of enthusiasm and scrummage well for the first twenty minutes then they lose both their concentration and the will to dominate. This is precisely where the side with the right attitude developed through concentrated practice can cash in.

Clubs must also accept that the value of tight-head ball has been grossly exaggerated largely by Press and television critics. How often do we read "x lost the scrums 3–nil". This proves precisely nothing because the pack which lost the tight-heads could have been pushing the other eight all over the field. The statisticians could, no doubt, quote the tight-head "score" in the Wales/England game 1971. Perhaps England won. Wales certainly did not because they hardly ever struck on the tight-head during the whole of the game. Perhaps England won but they were scrummaged out-of-existence; where is the meaning in the tight-head count now?

It is the *quality of ball* which counts and figures, as they are at present given, take no account of quality. If a team has the right attitude towards tight-head ball, the hooker will contribute much of the time to an eight-man shove and consequently the opposition ball (which they are nearly always going to get even if the opposing hooker strikes) is often of poor quality. One thus has the opportunity to put them under pressure.

Attitude by itself, however, is not enough, it must be allied to fitness and technique. Forwards must supplement the specific fitness for scrummaging developed largely through scrummaging practice by strength and power training. The easiest way to do this is by the use of weights. Most top-class forwards work on weights or are involved in heavy manual labour such as the Welsh miner and New Zealand farmer. But it must be admitted that the closure of many of the South Wales mines has reduced the supply of typically hard and resilient Welsh forwards. Let it be whispered too that New Zealand farms are becoming more automated!

The technique of scrummaging can be covered under three headings: foot positioning, snap shove and mechanics.

FOOT POSITIONING

Correct foot positioning is essential if the ball is to be produced cleanly and quickly. Figure 1 shows the correct foot positions. These, of course, can be modified provided an effective

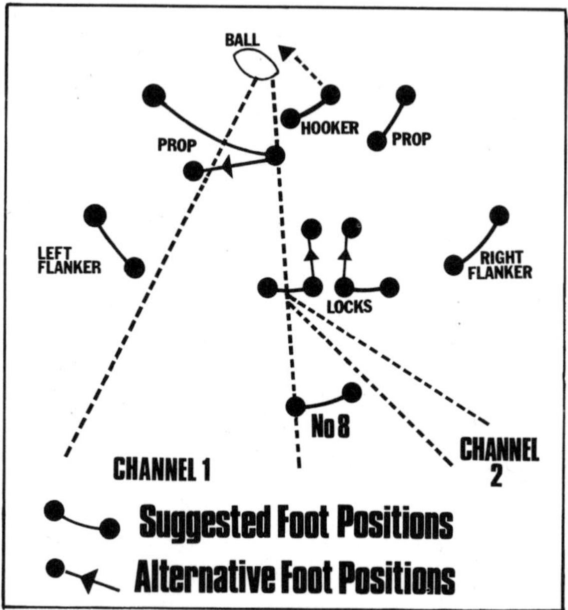

Figure 1

ball channel is left. There is often a good deal of argument about the best ball channel. Reference to Figure 1 shows two ball channels. Most teams disregard Channel 1 and go for Channel 2. This is to deny the excellence of Channel 1 provided the ball is struck cleanly quickly and under control. It demands high standards from both hooker and scrum-half but the reward is real quality possession.

If, on the other hand, the ball is slow in coming then Channel 2 must be used in order to protect the scrum-half. This is a good place for the scrum-half to pick up the ball but it is not necessarily good ball. Some sides, notably from New Zealand, when they want absolute control, perhaps on a wet day, often pack the Number 8 between the left lock and left flanker. In any event a good pack should be able to use either channel.

SNAP SHOVE

An explosive drive from seven or eight forwards is difficult to resist and it is a pre-requisite for quality possession. The key is "Snap" shove. It can be achieved as in

Figure 2 packing down with heads up, legs flexed and being absolutely steady. As the ball comes in, drive explosively with the legs and pull in with the arms. Keep driving forwards. It is an idea to get all eight forwards to shout "now" as the ball comes in, for this ensures good timing of the "Snap".

MECHANICS

A look at Figure 3 will clarify the mechanics of the 3–4–1 scrum. Briefly they are these: the props shove straight forwards; the hooker has no shoving responsibility, at least on his ball; the locks shove on the props; the flankers shove inwards to keep the props square; the No. 8 shoves straight with perhaps more emphasis on the right shoulder in order to counter act the tendency for the scrum to swing to the loose head side.

From this it is obvious that the flankers have an essential scrummaging role. They must, therefore, not play as breakaways for this much reduces the effectiveness of the pack.

There are some other important mechanical principles apart from the obvious ones, like flexed legs and straight backs. Two, in particular, are the use of the hands and arms and the position of the shoving shoulders. The importance of grip cannot be over-emphasised. It can be clearly illustrated by asking two packs to scrum down; then get one side to grip really tightly—the effect on the other side is quite remarkable.

Figure 2

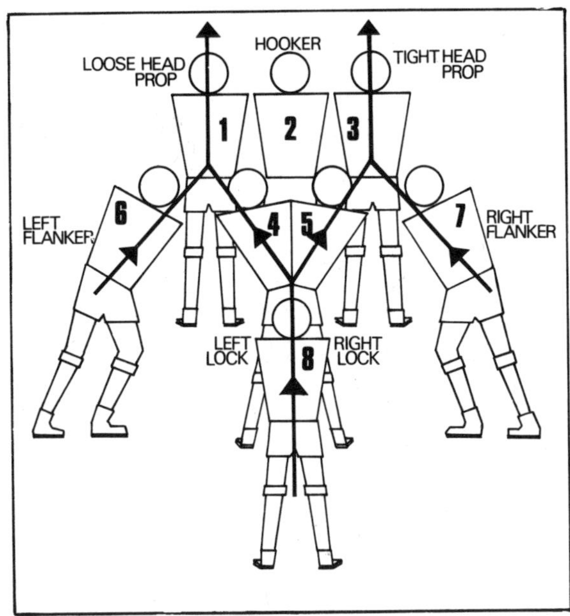

Figure 3

In connection with grip, a few words on the binding of locks on to props would not go amiss. Many locks now bind with the outside arm through the prop's legs. It is usually easier for the lock to bind like this and it leaves a clear area for the flanker's shoving shoulder. However, it is very doubtful whether it is as mechanically efficient as the outside arm binding around the prop. Locks should be encouraged to go for this latter position. There really is no problem for the flanker because all the lock has to do is to raise his outside elbow slightly and that exposes the correct shoving area for the flanker's shoulder.

As far as shoving shoulders are concerned, it is useless pushing them into the fleshy part of the buttock. When the real force is applied the shoulders will ride over on to the back and the shove is thus lost. The correct place is immediately below the buttock and this can easily be found by packing low on the thigh and allowing the shoulder to slide upwards. When it stops this is the right place, you might say, Nature's niche made for

Rugby forwards to shove against!

Occasionally even a good pack will meet a bigger and better pack. They may get pushed back both on their own and opposition ball. In such cases it is necessary to adopt the "lock" position. Figure 4 shows a good illustration. Heads must be up to ensure straight backs, hips low and legs straight. By using this technique the pack anchors itself and can prevent a much heavier pack pushing it off the ball.

The emphasis in this article has been on the collective contribution of the whole pack and it is right that this should be so. It would, therefore, be unfortunate to start stressing the role of particular individuals. It must, however, be understood that props are vitally important people, they must be able to transmit shove and resist it. There are those who say that the tight-head prop should be the strongest man in the team. This can

Figure 4

be countered by saying that the loose head is the most difficult position and perhaps he ought to be the strongest. *The real answer surely lies in the fact that both props must be strong—they cannot be too strong.*

What technique an individual may adopt, it must not transgress the general principles outlined above for the production or denial of quality possession, but, when all is said and done, the key factors in scrummaging are *shove, shove, shove!*

Clive Rowlands (Welsh Team Coach) runs a squad training session

English Schools Moves and Ploys

by Jack Priest

Jack Priest, the England Schoolboys' coach, sets down a few recent moves and ploys used with success by the England Schools 15 and 19 Group teams. Try and work out some of your own moves on similar lines, both in theory and practice.

Rugby football, like all other games, has changed much between 1965 and 1972. No longer are forwards referred to as "the dull eight" and backs as "the fairies". Today every player must be able to run, pass, sidestep, jink, kick and above all, *think*. He must be proficient at the many skills associated with his particular position.

Each member of the team should know and understand the techniques required to play in other positions. Attacking and defending plans and ploys must be known and practised by all members of the team. Every player should have a copy of his team's moves which he can study and learn. Here are a few of the successful moves and ploys used in some recent international matches by the English Schools' rugby teams.

Later you can try to work out some moves of your own on blank paper. But no theoretical moves are of the slightest use unless they can be proved successful on the field. In other words practice is worth a ton of theory.

Move A. Try from a Short Line-out

Hooker throws in. No. 1 kicks ball over goal-line. Hooker moves forward quickly to touch down for a try. To ensure success with this move, No. 1 must work a space between himself and the five-yards line. The hooker must bluff the opposition into thinking it is going to be a long line. He then throws the ball to the feet of No. 1 who side-foots the ball over the goal-line. The hooker moves forward and scores.

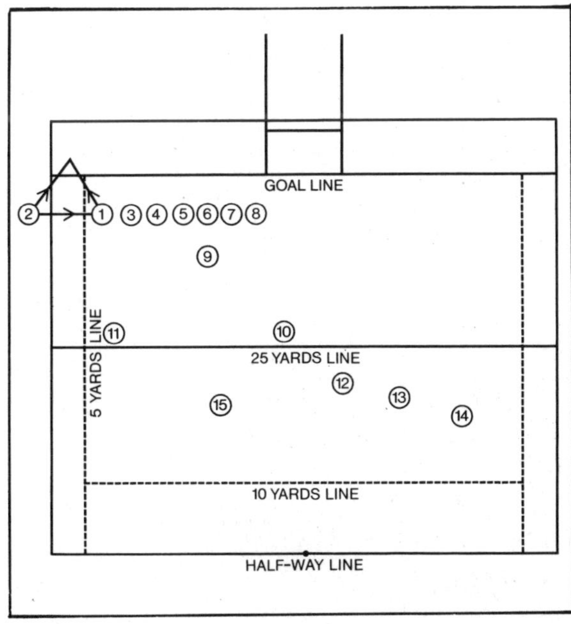

Move B. Drop Goal from a Scrum in front of the Posts

This move should only be used when a scrum is taking place directly in front of the posts and your scrum-half is putting the ball in. The captain will make a big fuss of bringing both wings into the scrum! They will shove on Nos. 4 and 5. The opposition will assume that a pushover try is being attempted. The extra weight of two men ensures a quick heel. No. 9 passes swiftly to No. 10 who drops a goal from his favoured position behind the scrum and in front of the posts.

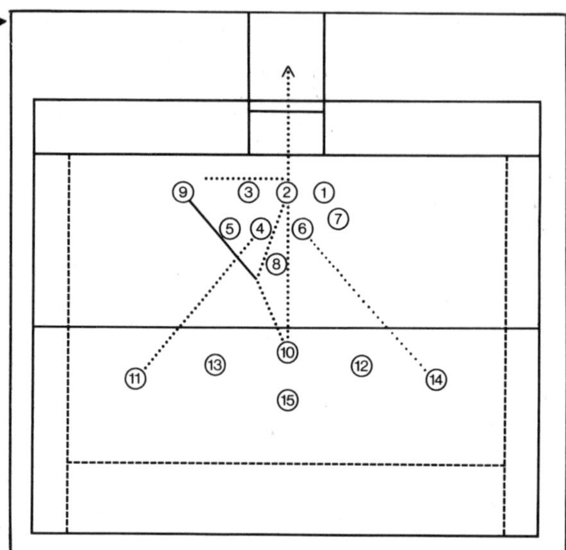

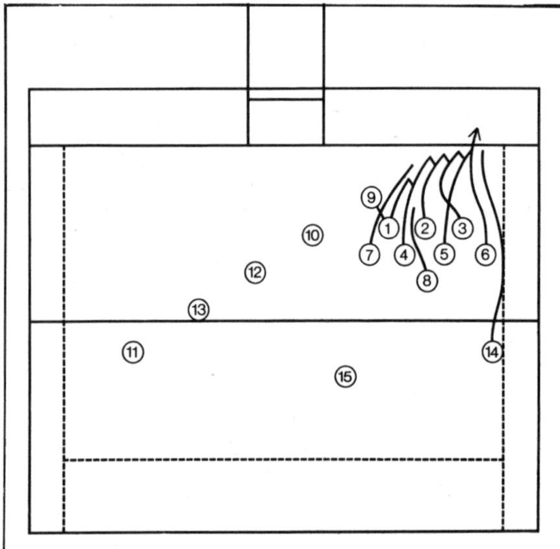

Move C. Try from a Short Penalty near the Goal-line

No. 9 dummies to his No. 10 and then passes inside to No. 1. When the forwards receive the ball they must move forward quickly with very short passes. It is most important that every forward when stopped drops his shoulder into his opponent, then turns his back on the opposition and gives the ball to the next forward. The ball must be kept moving at all times.

Move D. Try from a Line-out near the Goal-line

This move should be used when a line-out is taking place close to your own goal-line. No. 2 will throw the ball over the heads of the three line-out forwards. No. 9 collects the ball and starts a passing movement, using Nos. 7 and 8 who will link up with the backs. No. 11 is brought into the passing on the right-hand side of the field. The advantage of this move is that most sides will expect a defensive ploy from this position and will not guard against an attack. Also the opposition must be ten yards away from the line-out.

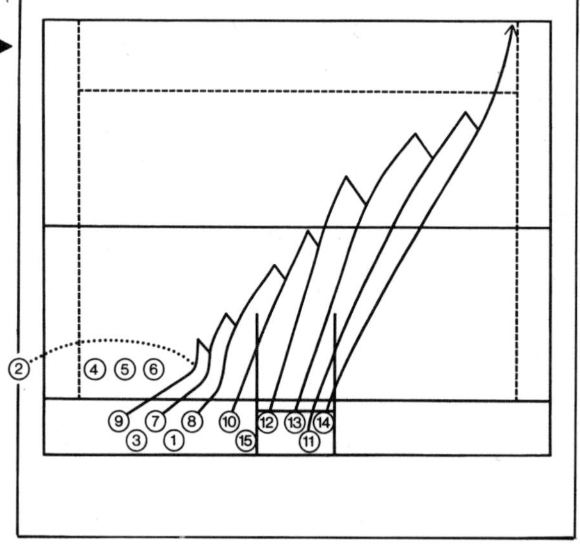

Budge Rogers in Bosuns' colours v P.S.W.

I have been intensely interested in the opening of new clubhouses ever since my Wolf Cub days in Manchester, when a highly respected solicitor clad in knee-length corduroy shorts took a running jump at the door of our new den armed with a huge felling-axe.

All he had to do was a fairly simple task—hacking his way through a mound of logs and then attacking the door until it burst open. The multitudes were then expected to cheer while a photographer from the local paper heaved up and down under his black cloak and tripod.

In fact the day was a near-disaster since the solicitor missed his target and disappeared from sight. Soon he was being transported away for medical attention. Later we heard he had ruptured himself, poor chap. Meanwhile the felling-axe remained in the door-frame, a silent testimony to honest endeavour.

I was reminded of that far-off day a year or so ago when I was invited to open a new clubhouse in North-West London. They handed me a fireman's axe to carry out the deed. Suitably, and movingly, inscribed with my name, as a memento of the occasion, it is still in my possession as a valued trophy. The idea was that I should use it to cut a silken cord tied across the clubhouse door. But the axe was so blunt we had to borrow a pair of nail scissors. One feels such a fool on these occasions. But it *is* an honour to be asked.

On the whole rugby clubhouse openings tend to be rather dreary and stereotyped affairs. I hope the Centenary season of the Rugby Union inspired a touch of glamour for future occasions. I can well imagine our distinguished Sir Bill Ramsay arriving by helicopter at the chosen site, then descending by rope ladder on to the modern ghastly flat roof which so many clubs now go in for, finally disappearing through some aperture and at length opening the clubhouse door from the inside and inviting everybody in. What we need is a touch of real originality.

I once attended the opening of a new cricket pavilion at a well-known school in the North. The guest of honour was the Lord Lieutenant of the county at the time, a gentleman of robust and ample proportions who would have caused a sensation if he had merely approached the door at speed, allowing one or other of his noble paunches to make contact and spring it open. Simple and natural.

But protocol demanded that the task should be carried out formally with a golden key following a long and very dreary speech with little relevance to the occasion. The golden key stuck firmly and obstinately. It would neither come out nor open the door. The door, naturally, wouldn't budge an inch. The Sixth Form, standing expressionless in the back row of the stalls, had seen to that alright.

The headmaster, pink and flustered, immediately ordered the groundsman to break in at the rear of the pavilion and undo the door from the inside, crawling on his stomach as he did so to avoid detection. Alas, the groundsman had as much difficulty getting in the back door as the Lord Lieutenant had at the front door. There was a horrifying crash of broken glass as he climbed in through the showers window. When at length he did arrive at the pavilion door it was seen he was almost covered in whitewash. To the dismay of all the hierarchy he was heard to mouth quite loudly a choice selection of strange oaths picked up during his World War I service in the Egyptian Camel Corps.

As far as the Sixth Form were concerned it was a huge success. I would rather not say what the Lord Lieutenant said.

Now let us turn to the prophets of the Old Testament and see what they have to say about clubhouses. "There are many doors in every temple . . ." we read. All, in my opinion, need to be opened with due ceremony. It is no use opening just one door in a clubhouse and then saying "Well, here you are, chaps! Get in, start drawing the pints and don't forget to save one for me . . ."

Every door needs to be opened with due ritual. A suitable one is the hurling of one pint of ale across the door in question before it is formally declared open. Impress upon all concerned that the actual glasses or tankards should not be hurled as well. Ale used in door-opening ceremonies need not be sound drinkable stuff or, indeed, any good, swift-selling brew in demand. We live in inflationary times and therefore clubs must endeavour to save money.

There are sure to be quantities of revolting bottled ales which have been in the Ladies' Bar for years, the kind of stuff that strongly resembles a good old Northern mouthwash known as sarsaparilla. The clubhouse opening is an ideal time to clear out old stocks and charge them up to Miscellaneous Expenses.

When opening the internal doors of new clubhouses on the great day it is important to ensure that the rooms or offices concerned are not actually occupied. This applies especially to the Ladies, and the Gentlemen's, Powder Rooms. A bottle of old rubbish thrown carelessly in the face or lap of someone likely to give you 20 guineas a year if asked nicely could be disastrous to the club, and very hard to explain when the loss of income is discussed at next season's Annual General Meeting.

Finally, a note of caution. On the great day you are sure to have a guest XV of enormous strength, possibly all Internationals, opposing your miserable club side reinforced for the day with a few old County has-beens of doubtful vintage. Do not be dismayed. There will be plenty of last-minute changes in the opposition and the printer of the programme should leave plenty of space around each name for the inevitable changes. Unless you are playing in a rich smog they cannot exceed fifteen. But do watch the opposition. They will drink everything in sight if given half a chance, and steal all your cars and your women as well.

The abounding secret of success in modern rugby is the art of never, and I must repeat, *never*, allowing your braces to dangle.

"*Do they call this* **rugby**? *They're like a lot of tame rabbits.*"

◀ *A line-out in the England & Wales v Scotland & Ireland 1970–71 Centenary Match at Twickenham*

▼ *New Zealand v Wales (2nd. Test) at Auckland on June 14, 1969*

Firestone
TYRES
DOWN WITH
GUINNESS
DB
TODAYS
GREAT
DRINK
FIRST IN

Internationals on Five Saturdays Only

by J. B. G. Thomas

AFTER the 1971-72 season during which the New Zealand All Blacks are due to make a tour of the British Isles, the Four Home Unions have agreed, and indeed published, a fixture list for at least ten seasons ahead, providing a rotation of fixtures. This means that Scotland v France and England v Wales will no longer be the regular opening matches of each international domestic season in Europe.

It was suggested in the 1950s with a scheme drawn up for the consideration of the Home Countries by the late Vincent Griffiths, one of the best and most popular selectors produced by the Principality in the post-war years. At the time the scheme was rejected because Scotland did not desire to move the time-honoured date of the Calcutta Cup match because on the day, the third Saturday in March each year, many meetings and events were held and rugby followers attending such meetings also wanted to watch the Calcutta Cup match.

It seemed an unusual excuse and friendly pressure was brought to bear upon Scotland and eventually her agreement was obtained with the proviso that such a rotation did not start until after the Centenary Celebrations of the two Rugby Unions of England. This was agreed and as the New Zealanders are due to tour in the next season, a start will be made in 1973–74. In that season there will be five Saturdays devoted to international matches in the months of January, February and March. This means that on all five days there will be two matches, and the international season will be condensed.

One of my closest friends in the Press Box and as true a follower as anyone I know, Vivian Jenkins, is much against rotation because he says it will prevent any person wanting to see all or most of the international matches in a season. Obviously, this is a valid point and not to be dismissed easily, but I do feel the call of the bigger clubs is worthy of consideration.

The fly in the ointment and a means for good and evil is television. When the season is spread over eight Saturdays with seven of them, and possibly more, affected by live TV, the big clubs suffer with poor gates. The idea of BBC 2 is an excellent one with the 7.30 p.m. showing, which does a considerable amount for the game and its players.

The live TV of Saturday afternoons, though it brings large sums of money to the four Home Unions, does affect gates and while the majority of clubs in all Unions may not take gate moneys, the bigger clubs are the show pieces and developing grounds for international players and cannot be ignored.

Thus the original plan of Vincent Griffiths, submitted by the W.R.U., was to curtail the number of Saturdays affected by international calls and TV programmes live. Players and officials have been concerned in recent years at the demands of representative rugby upon clubs. When one thinks of the rare appearances of Barry John and Gareth Edwards for Cardiff through injuries and the demands of representative matches, it is easy to see why the big clubs will welcome the rotation system and the limited international season.

However, there was a magnificent burst of representative football in 1971 as England and Scotland celebrated their centenaries in noble style and no one would have wished them to do otherwise. It was a notable year in the game and the first international match of March 27, 1871 at the Academy Ground, Edinburgh must have been a great one.

The provisional agreement for 1973–74 is that the five Saturdays will be as follows— 3rd Saturday in January: France v Ireland and Wales v Scotland; 1st Saturday in February: Ireland v Wales and Scotland v England; 3rd Saturday in February: Wales v France and England v Ireland; 1st Saturday in March: France v England and Ireland v Scotland; and 3rd Saturday in March: England v Wales and Scotland v France.

From these special dates, which will be continued each year except during visit of touring team when changes may be made, and will be standard Saturdays for each season. Clubs will know when they can avoid important club matches, or play them on Friday nights or Saturday mornings, so as not to clash with TV or international match demands.

It will be seen, too, that the interest in the Triple Crown will be maintained from first Saturday to last and that it could be decided with the Championship on the last of the Saturdays.

Whatever criticism may be laid at this innovation, and I happen to be in favour of it although it will curtail my viewing as a critic, it is a good idea. Again one word to BBC planners, for they could show a recording at 7.30 p.m. of one of the two matches for 45 minutes and another on Sunday afternoon, or a full showing on Saturday afternoon of one match, and a tele-recording of the other on Saturday evening.

As there are five Saturdays, and the clubs warned well in advance, I feel that there should be plenty of TV on these five days at, of course increased fees! At the moment, well-meaning though it may be, the box does encroach rather too much. One cannot have all sports on the telly and only a small number of spectators watching actual events!

I can imagine the second rugby man on each leading newspaper rubbing his hands with glee and saying, "T'is an ill wind . . .", because two rugby writers from each paper will be in action. Again, the top writers may only have one visit per season to each of the four cities away from London, in Paris, Dublin, Edinburgh and Cardiff!

So my advice to all and sundry, who feel they will be affected by the revolutionary change already in force in association football so as not to interfere with club football, is to make the most of it. While we must look after the showpiece of the game, we must also protect the clubs. The smaller clubs are happy families and will survive easily, but it is the bigger clubs that need protection. Rotation will be a big help for them.

Newport make an exciting break against London Welsh at the Old Deer Park, Richmond

Welsh Influences on French Rugby

by David Frost

The superb French flair for attractive, attacking rugby owes much to the influence and coaching of three Welshmen, Gwyn Nicholls, Owen Roe and Rowland Griffiths, who set the pattern of play.

When they are in real form, when they are true to themselves, the French can delight us with their impulsive running and passing, with their flair for attack, and with the apparently effortless way in which the whole side, forwards, half-backs, threequarters, and full-back, combine in sweeping movements, sometimes from deep inside their own half of the field.

The histories of the game tell us that rugby reached the French in the nineteenth century through commerce in the Channel ports with English businessmen, especially those engaged in the wine trade. It is not so well-known that the Welsh, too, played a vital role in the development of the game in the early days in France.

An occasion of far-reaching significance occurred in April 1913. That was when the final of the French club championship in Paris resulted in a win for Bayonne over S.C.U.F. *(Sporting Club Universitaire de France)* by the humiliating score of 33–8.

It was not just the size of the score, not even the exciting manner of it, that attracted attention. The point was that the rugby club

Dawes and John Williams fail to stop French Scrum-half Pebeyre scoring for the President's XV v Wales at Cardiff in the 1970–71 Centenary Match

at Bayonne had been founded only seven years before, in 1906. Starting from scratch, Bayonne had developed a fluid style of play which by 1913 had proved too good for all the long-established clubs in France. On the way to that final, in particular, they had had to meet Bordeaux, who had already been champions of France in eight different seasons. Bayonne's running and passing overcame the tight, traditional forward game of Bordeaux by a score of 9–0. It was the first home defeat ever suffered by the Bordeaux club in a championship match.

So by the time the Bayonne side travelled up to Paris for the final they had already caught the imagination of the French rugby public. When they won that final 33–8, their exploits were envied and analysed throughout the rugby-playing areas of France.

It was found that Bayonne had come under Welsh influence in two ways. In the first place one of the Bayonne members, on a visit to Britain, had met and talked at great length with Gwyn Nicholls, the centre who captained Wales in their famous victory over the All Blacks in 1905. Nicholls preached the value of the running and passing game; a book by him found its way back to the Bayonne club.

Then a member of the Penarth club, Owen Roe, settled in Bayonne and not only coached the club in the methods of threequarter play he had witnessed in the "Golden Era" of Welsh rugby but also played in their matches. Thus the Basques of Bayonne, under the indirect influence of Nicholls and the direct influence of Roe, discovered a style of joyous rugby ideally suited to their temperament and to their natural talent as ball-players. Basques have a natural agility and dexterity deriving from countless games of their beloved *pelota* played as kids against the village walls.

When Owen Roe's coaching harnessed these instinctive Basque skills to the disciplines of Welsh threequarter play, the result was devastating for the rugby clubs elsewhere in France. Roe himself had the pleasure of taking part in that final of 1913. Thereafter the Bayonne style was not only envied but copied extensively, and there is little doubt that April 1913 marks the beginning of the modern French game which in later years became so much admired and respected.

Curiously, while Roe was instructing his Bayonne players at the Atlantic end of the Pyrenees, another Welshman, Rowland Griffiths, was busy at the Mediterranean end, at Perpignan. Griffiths settled at Perpignan in 1912 and became captain of the local rugby club. Under his guidance the Catalans of Perpignan were introduced to the mysteries of Welsh threequarter play in much the same way as Roe was teaching the Basques.

It was surely more than a coincidence that the club who followed Bayonne as champions of France in 1914 were Perpignan!

THE WANDERERS QUIZ

Here are Ten football clubs which have the distinguished appellation "Wanderers" added on to the name given. (We have not included the famous Irish rugby club Wanderers in this Quiz.) But one of the clubs included is no longer known under the title we have given. Name the Rugby Union clubs and the odd club out.
1. Edinburgh 2. Ilford 3. Public Schools
4. Wolverhampton 5. Shirley 6. Thanet
7. Deal 8. Berkshire 9. Bolton
10. Glamorgan

Solution on Page 93

Quoro wins a line-out for Fiji v Junior All-Blacks, Wellington 1970

Another line-out in the Cambridge University v Fiji Match, 1970

by Vivian Jenkins

"Fijian magic" was a phrase that hit many a headline during England's 1970–71 season. Fiji brought colour and excitement to the Rugby Union's Centenary season. No one will ever forget the sheer exuberance of their open play.

It was an inspired thought on someone's part to invite these wonderfully gay, exciting players to make a tour at a time when celebration, not dour, win-at-all-costs Rugby, was to be the order of the day. And how splendidly the visitors rose to the occasion. They may not have won all their matches—indeed their record, P.14. W.6. D.1. L.7. Pts. for 168, Pts. Agst. 165, was only average; but their style of play, and their attitude towards the game, won them countless friends throughout the length and breadth of the country. "Our aim" said their manager, Ratu Penaiya Ganilau, at the beginning of the tour "will be to win with modesty, lose with dignity, and above all keep our country's proud name in the game unsoiled". That aim, he can be assured, was more than fulfilled. From first to last the tourists played the open, attacking game, with the ball being flung about in all directions, and forwards joining in with their backs in movements that surged from one end of the field to the other. From time to time, too, they produce huge, flamboyant one-handed passes right across the field which completely altered the direction of the

Friends

Fiji's scrum-half Batibusaga in Action v Midland Counties at Coventry

attack, and thrilled the big crowds who watched them. "It may not be disciplined, method rugby, as the All Blacks play it" said their assistant manager Dr. Felix Emberson, "but it is our style of rugby, and we do not intend to change it. Nor can we, even if we wished. I spent five years in New Zealand as a player, and tried to introduce their methods, as a coach, to my club in Suva when I returned; but after ten minutes the players returned to their natural style. It is what they want to do. The difference is also reflected in their attitude to winning. Win-

ning is not really important to Fiji teams. They accept victory and defeat in the same light. For this reason they will probably never become the greatest team in the world. They don't think on those lines. Their conscious objective is the game—to play it their way and to enjoy it."

Where could one hope to find a better blue-print for the right attitude to rugby than that? The cult of win-at-all-costs "hate the opposition" rugby, with the game closed up like a clam if necessary, seems very stale, flat and unprofitable by comparison. The Fijians not only enjoyed their own rugby on their way round Britain. They also gave untold pleasure to the millions who watched them on television, as well as those who went to the grounds. Yet the odd thing is that there were quite a lot of people, afterwards, who were ready to write down their performance. There were even those who tried to find an excuse for England's 22–6 defeat against Wales at Cardiff in the fact that eight of the England Under-25 team which had beaten the Fijians 15–11 at Twickenham were included for the senior international. "After all" it was argued "The Fijians weren't all that good, were they?". The implication was that the selectors had erred in attaching so much importance to the win by their Under-25 team.

What puzzled me about this was the lack of appreciation of how amazingly good the Fijians were considering their lack of facilities, and numbers, at home. People judged them by our own standards here, which are in no way related.

There are, in fact, only about 200,000 Fijians inhabiting the 300 or so islands, covering 300,000 square miles of the Pacific Ocean, which go to make up their country. The rest of the population of under half a

million is made up of over 240,000 Indians, who outnumber the Fijians, and some 40,000 others. But it is only the indigenous Fijians who play Rugby, and out of their total of 200,000, male and female, there are probably only 15,000 or so males between the ages of 20 and 30 from whom to pick their side. It is fantastic, in the circumstances, that they can produce a team capable of challenging, if not beating, the best in the world. It was, indeed, a remarkable performance that they were able to beat the Barbarians, including fourteen home internationals, by 29 pts. to 9 at Gosforth. In the process they produced a display of running and sleight of hand that had the crowd in ecstasies. The more one considers their background, the more remarkable it seems. "The Fijians are natural athletes" said a pre-tour hand-out by a London public relations agency. "From the time they learn to walk around their village, or thatched houses, they develop rippling muscles, precise co-ordination, keen eyesight and enduring strength. They live an outdoor life, much of it close to the sea. Every Fijian male leaps joyfully into team games on the village green from the age of about five. He swims like a dolphin even before that. He's out spearing fish on the reef as a small lad. He learns seamanship from the sound of the waves against his outrigger canoe, and by keen observation of the small passage through the tumbling coral reef. Every facet of his life combines to fashion him into a natural athlete. If he pulls a muscle during practice, he rubs it with coconut oil, sometimes improved with aromatic herbs." And so on, with a reference to the "contentment, tranquillity and fun" of life in Fiji, the abundance of fresh fish and tropical fruits,

◀ *Fiji's War Dance at Cambridge University, 1970, was a preliminary!*

which help to build up the Fijians' natural physique. That they are hard as nails was abundantly demonstrated during their matches. So much so, indeed, that there were occasions, notably at Gloucester against Gloucestershire and Somerset, when there were injuries galore. Several of the home team were "in the wars", with hooker John Pullin needing 15 stitches in three cuts on his head, fly-half Gabitass suffering a depressed fracture of the cheekbone, prop-forward Rodgers being concussed in a clash of heads in the scrum, and scrum-half Spalding handicapped throughout with a painful rib injury. The Fijians themselves also had to call on two substitutes—as had the home team, for Pullin and Rodgers—and fly-half George Barley and lock-forward Jope Naucabalavu both had to be replaced. So the damage was mutual.

Yet in most of the cases they were the result of the sheer exuberance and gusto of the Fijians' play, and their hardness, rather than foul play. In the few cases where indiscretions occured, they stemmed from frustration on the Fijians' part at differences in interpretation of the laws from those which they were used to at home. Later in the tour, indeed, Ratu Penaiya Ganilau, their manager, complained about referees failing to check obstruction in the line-out and not strictly applying the law relating to players rolling away from the ball. The difficulties occur on almost every major tour, and by the end the Fijians had adapted themselves much better. But they were still apt to incur penalties through over-eagerness, and impetuosity, rather than malice aforethought. Still, if they had not been like that, we should have been deprived of all the other delights in their play. Their one aim, after all, was to run with the ball, and how splendidly they lived up to

Fiji's outstanding prop, Quoro, tearing through Western Counties

all, but unfortunately had to miss most of the matches through injury; George Barley and Isimeli Batibasaga, a fine pair of halves, with Batibasaga the side's best goalkicker; and Ilaitia Tuisese and Vuniani Varo, both loose-forwards, in an astonishingly mobile pack. The side's line-out work and set-scrummaging was not up to the standard of most of the teams they met, but they made ample amends by their devastating play in the loose. Another feature of their play which the crowds loved was their switching of the direction of the attack by those huge, one-handed passes right across the field. Sometimes these went astray, and cost them tries, but it made no difference to their attitude. If the same kind of situation occurred, they would do it again, and more likely than not, this time, it would end in a try. "We cannot alter our style of play", said Dr. Emberson. "The New Zealanders have their method, and you have yours, but winning is not everything. Our chief conscious objective is the game itself—to play it our way and to enjoy it." The Fijians have since been inundated with invitations to play all over the world. Enjoyment on the part of the players has a way of transmitting itself to those watching as well.

their "credo" in this respect. Every one of their forwards could run like a back, and it was a sight to see vast men like Nasive Ravouvou, their 6 ft. 3 ins. lock, and Jona Qoro, their 16 st. lock, careering about the field like wings. Qoro, indeed, must be in world class in his position, and was rated as such by many New Zealanders when the team toured there before coming on to England.

Other players who impressed were Josaia Visei, a running full-back whose side-step would have put that of most fly-halves to shame; Pio Tikoisuva, who scored some outstanding tries on the left wing; Kiniviliame Nalatu, a centre who looked their best back of

My own abiding memory of the tour will not be of any particular incident, but of the gnarled smiling face of their big lock-forward and vice-captain, Jope Naucabalavu, with his splendid drooping moustache. I doubt if I have ever seen anyone who gave the appearance of enjoying the game more, and the tougher the exchanges were the more likely he was to come out of them with a huge grin all over his face. If any of the younger players became over-excited at any time, too, he was quick to calm them down with a deprecatory wave of his hands, like a father

soothing his flock. Top rugby could certainly do with more of his kind.

In Sum, the Fijians left a host of friends behind them, just as they did on their previous visit, to Wales in 1964. Their manager Ratu Penaiya Ganilau, son of an hereditary chief, was a most impressive man. A former Fijian international forward himself, he won the D.S.O. in 1956 as commander of a Fijian infantry battalion, and is now his country's Minister of Defence. The captain of the touring side, Sela Toga, a No. 8 forward, also did a worthy job, and met victory and defeat with equal dignity.

One thing that affected the team's performance in its later matches was the cold weather—so different from their "60 degrees to 90 degrees" at home. Indeed, 60 degrees, by them, is regarded as "distinctly chilly". After their match against England Under-25 at Twickenham, on a bitterly cold day, the entire team jumped into the hot bath with all their kit on, including their boots! Next time, perhaps, they should end their tour a little sooner.

As it is, they provided just the kind of fare needed to give spice to England's Centenary celebrations, "They ran with the ball" could be their epitaph, and they will be more than welcome whenever they return.

FIX THE FIXTURES

Here is a list of Saturday fixtures between genuine football teams, and the majority of them are Rugby Union teams. Check each one and then decide which fixtures could be Rugby Union matches. Time Limit: Ten Minutes!

1. Sheffield Wednesday v Leicester Thursday
2. Plymouth Albion v West Bromwich Albion
3. Torquay Athletic v Bedford Athletic
4. Cardiff Athletic v Bristol United
5. Edinburgh Wanderers v Coventry
6. Hartlepool Rovers v Bristol Rovers
7. Newquay Hornets v Rochdale Hornets
8. Durham City v Swansea City
9. Arsenal v School of Mines
10. Metropolitan Police v Anti-Assassins
11. Wellington Hornets v Swindon
12. Wolverhampton v Sutton United
13. Royal Veterinary College v Oxford Greyhounds
14. Chester v Widnes
15. British Lions v "The Tigers" (Leicester)

Solution on Page 94

"The Ladies' God Bless 'em"

by Tony Lewis

The emancipation of women in the male theatre of Rugby football has been the greatest female triumph since the suffragettes won the vote

Traditionally their role was servile. Someone to wring out the mud from woollen socks in readiness for Saturday; a lackey to scrub football laces and dry them flat, so they didn't turn out all twisted on Saturday; someone to pocket false teeth as you ran onto the pitch for battle; to dutifully cheer whenever you went near the ball. She knew her place. Standing on the touchline she had to be warmly and sensibly clothed—not too glamorous, because the sight of glamour always extracted heroic effort from the opposition, and often resulted in your side getting a hammering!

Saturday night was man's night. Sausage and mash, pork pies and pasties, beer swilling endlessly from enamel jugs, rugby talk limitless, sinful songs and perhaps a conclusion of 'Cardinal Puff' or 'Buzz'. Only at this late stage on a Saturday night would one consider calling to see a girlfriend. Yes, on Saturday after the match, women

were 'optional extras'. One devoted young wife stuck to her lot so diligently that she used to go round on Sunday morning to pubs and club-houses recovering vital parts of her husband's wardrobe!

Well, those days have gone, and how militant the women were in cracking the male stronghold. 'Taff' Evans, a loyal clubman with Birmingham Welsh, was told by his wife to hang up his boots—*or else!* He cheated, and played without her knowing. Unfortunately his kit, which only came out on Saturday afternoons and was otherwise incarcerated in the boot of his car, was so dirty and carried such a fearful smell that he could not find anyone to pack down with him in the end. He was out of the game, and a woman had caused it!

What a shattering sight it was, too, to see Islwyn 'Rock', as he was called in school, walking a girl to the pictures on a Saturday night in Neath, after the match, *carrying her*

Olive Compton, wife of Wasps' President Neville Compton, is hostess at Sudbury, Middlesex

umbrella! If you could have seen him prop . . . still a schoolboy, but with a man's physique . . . you would understand. Born to prop was Islwyn, legs to support a grand piano, neckless and rock-hard. Mind you, his nickname, 'Rock', did not derive from his build. It happened that one night in the Dulais Rock Hotel (he was in Form 6 then) Islwyn drank a yard of Evans Bevan bitter with a bob's worth of pennies in his mouth! Fantastic. From then on he rightfully assumed the name of the pub.

But then that shattering sight in Neath. Here was my hero, who had left a trail of schoolboy prop forwards mangled in his wake. I was convinced he could have rubbed a respectable shoulder against Neath's British Lion, Courtenay Meredith, yet he was walking sedately to the pictures when there was a great sing-song building up in his rugby club. Eve had conquered once again.

That's all history now. Go into a rugby club these days and there's a lady to serve you a pint, another to produce a hot pasty, fifty to sell you a raffle ticket! Schooners of sherry, gins and tonic, brandy and American —no longer the standing order of fifteen pints. Of course, not only have the ladies broken in, they have become totally indispensable to the modern clubhouse and its finances.

Richmond Rugby Club saw all this happening early on, so they committed the shower-room song-cycle to posterity on record; the old songs may never be sung (or performed) again, live.

But the most complete female take-over in rugby football is at Aberavon, where the now famous Mrs. Mainwaring dictates the actual playing tactics from her seat in the grandstand right behind the committee box. Her son, an international and club captain, a formidable rugby thinker in his own right, is left in no doubt as to what he should be doing at every minute of the game. So loud is Mam's voice it not only safely carries to play on the other side of the field, but some say the sheer volume has caused soil erosion on

'Shipwreck Night' at the Colwyn Bay Rugby Club

the mountainside which skirts the far touch-line. '*Kick*', she shouts, and the man in possession dutifully applies the boot. Then the most uncompromising female instruction, '*Get stuck in, Afan*'—and woe betide the shirkers of Aberavon.

But if you still have a yen for the all-male rugby fraternity then take a Friday rail excursion from Cardiff to Edinburgh for international day. I recall seeing swarms of fans in 1970 at all the pick-up stations unloading barrels and cans of beer onto the train off hand-carts and barrows. I reckoned there were 1,500 supporters, 15,000 pints, and one solitary girl on that bulging train. But do you know, when that attractive young lady moved through our midst to the dining car—red maxi coat, white boots and white scarf, she brought the whole male charade to a halt. 'Come on, Wales', they shouted at her. She loved it, to the rather taut non-amusement of her husband. I felt like going up to him and passing on the old truth: 'Dress them warmly and sensibly, mate. Glamour extracts too much effort from the opposition.' Even with odds of one against 1,500, the women will win in the end. God bless 'em!

THE PARK QUIZ

Here are Fourteen clubs which have the word "Park" added on to the name given to form the full name of the club. Usually, but not always, this denotes the origin of the club or its past or present home ground. Two of the clubs, however, are fictitious but are genuine parks not unassociated with Rugby Union football. Can you name them?

1. Broughton 2. Westcombe 3. Birkenhead
4. Romford and Gidea 5. Rosslyn
6. Winnington 7. Cassiobury 8. West
9. Sedgley 10. Stockwood 11. Mowden
12. Percy 13. Charlton 14. Heaton

Solution on Page 93

Inflation Hits London Rugby Hard

by Jack Cox

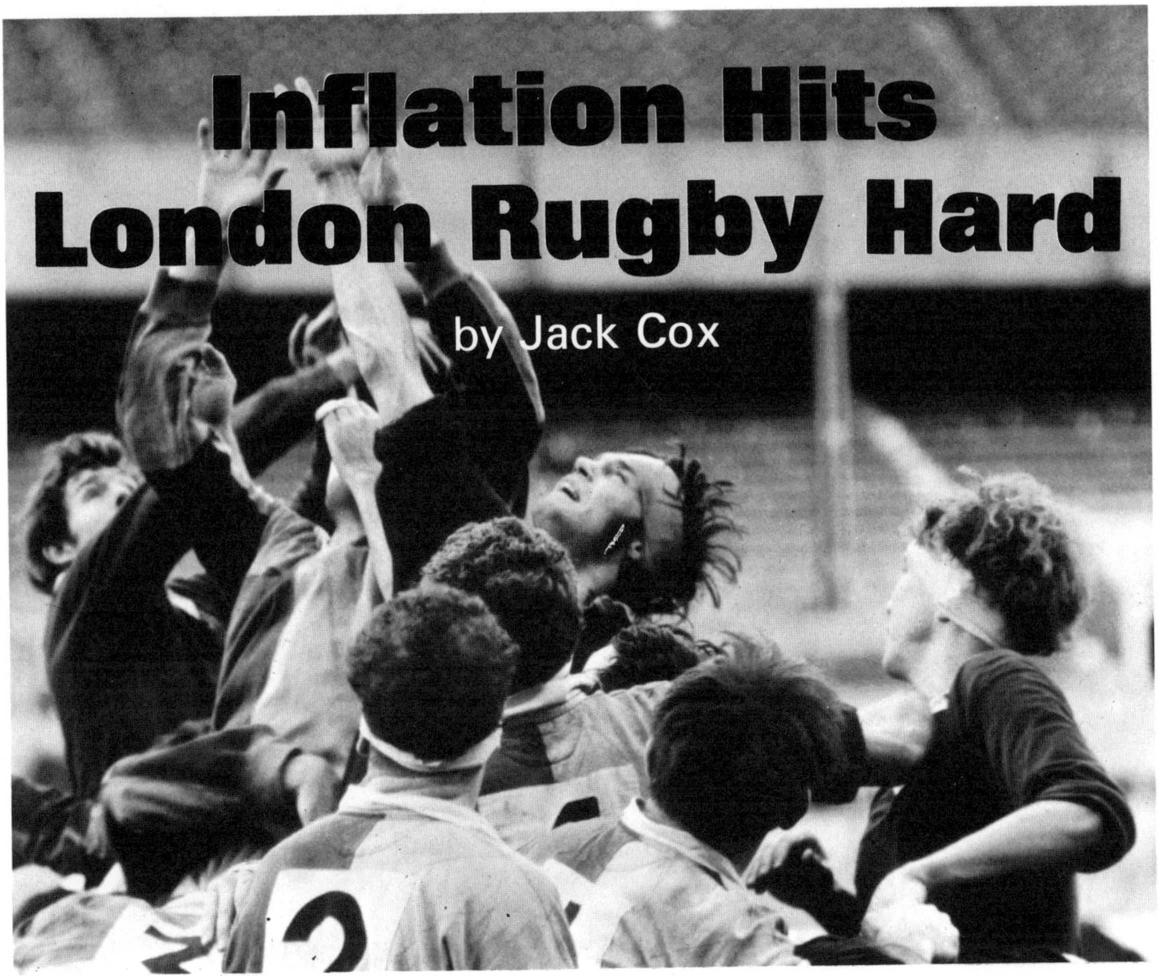

Hayward (Harlequins) wins the ball from Oxford University

Players no longer stay in London for very long, thanks to high all-round costs, transport and parking problems and opportunities overseas. This may explain the current lack of talent in many of our London clubs today.

One disturbing feature of the Centenary season 1970–71 was the marked decline of London rugby in the playing sense. Some of the strongest and best clubs in the game can be found in the Metropolis. They are well-organised, have splendid grounds, clubhouses and facilities, excel in the important social side of the game and are progressive in every sense of the word. Yet the capacity of London clubs to attract talent from other parts of the country, or to develop it themselves, seems to be on the wane.

What is the reason for this state of affairs? After a probing enquiry I can only come to one conclusion: the main reason is inflation, or at least the inflationary process. Before I discuss this further let us have a look at the playing records of senior London clubs in the Centenary season of the Rugby Union. Writing in mid-January, 1971 I could only make a comparison from September 1, 1970, to January 9, 1971, but it is sufficient to illustrate the situation.

Leaving aside the important question of

relative fixture strengths for a moment we see that only six senior clubs had any cause for celebration. If we take the number of wins as a yardstick the order of merit at the time of writing was:

	Won	Drawn	Lost
London Irish	16	0	2
London Welsh	15	2	3
London Scottish	14	1	6
Met. Police	12	0	7
Streatham/Croydon	12	1	9
Saracens	11	1	7

The remaining seven senior clubs' records presented a dismal picture. Here it is:

	Won	Drawn	Lost
Harlequins	8	1	7
Rosslyn Park	7	2	10
Blackheath	6	0	11
Wasps	5	0	14
Richmond	4	1	11
Guy's Hospital	3	0	15
Esher	3	3	16

A club of near-senior status, Sidcup, were once more in the lead at the half-way stage, with 17 wins and 5 losses, but Woodford had only 7 wins from 15 games and Sutton 6 wins from 16 games.

The "Old Boys" sides were faring equally badly. Only the Bancroftians with 15 wins from 17 games and Whitgiftians, with 13 wins from 20 games, had a good showing. Millhillians could claim only 5 wins from 16 games, OMT 6 from 16.

The Hospitals were pretty much the same. Guy's, the only one with a senior fixture list, had but 3 wins from 18 games but London Hospital, as usual, were doing much better with 15 wins from 23. Mary's, once the pride of London with wartime crowds of several

40

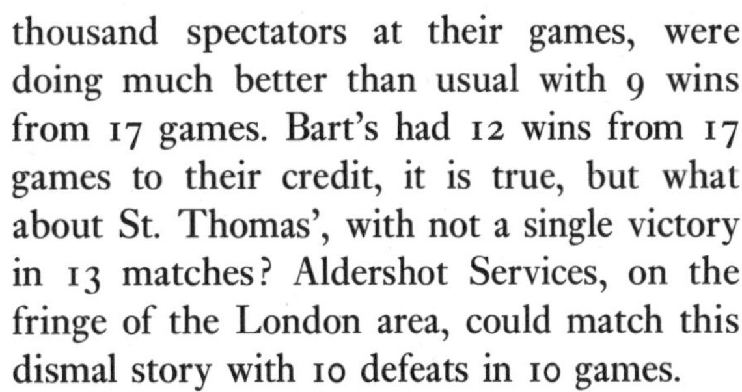

thousand spectators at their games, were doing much better than usual with 9 wins from 17 games. Bart's had 12 wins from 17 games to their credit, it is true, but what about St. Thomas', with not a single victory in 13 matches? Aldershot Services, on the fringe of the London area, could match this dismal story with 10 defeats in 10 games.

One of the great difficulties in assessing any relative performances by senior clubs is the varying strength of fixture lists. In London Harlequins and Wasps have the strongest fixtures of all so that if they are doing badly they will show up very badly against, say, London Irish, whose list is a very mixed one. Saracens and Streatham/ Croydon are strengthening their lists all the time; sooner or later they are going to say "No" to a number of old friends, which is always a difficult one to face in rugby, where fixtures are personally-arranged encounters between friends.

The Exiles are all doing well and none of them lack reserve talent in depth. Accomplished Welsh, Irish and Scottish players seem to arrive in London with disturbing regularity. As one player drops out with injury someone else is posted to the Metropolis almost at once to take his place. I cannot explain this phenomenon at all! I do not know how it is done. It just seems to happen. Perhaps the Exile clubs are a race apart, a sort of semi-permanent International trial arrangement against the English? I only wish we had comparable English sides playing in Cardiff, Edinburgh and Dublin. It may seem strange to think of Newport or Llanelli playing Cardiff English, or West of Scotland playing Edinburgh English but it

Spawforth, talented Army and Rosslyn Park scrum-half, in action at Roehampton

might not be a bad idea at all.

Yet there are anomalies in the Exiles fixture lists. The Scottish play London Welsh, but never Newport, Cardiff or Llanelli. Yet Harlequins, Wasps and Blackheath have five or six fixtures each season against Newport, Cardiff, Llanelli and Swansea. The Irish play Aberavon but also Old Alleyians, OMT, Osterley, Oxford (the town club), US Portsmouth, Guy's, St. Mary's and St. Thomas' Hospitals. Well as they play, their fixture list is not comparable with other leading London clubs. The Scottish would be a more glamorous side if they played more powerful provincial clubs as well as leading Welsh ones.

It is one thing to have a powerful fixture list built up over many years by dedicated club officials who know that the big clubs, the real backbone of the game, need gate-money urgently to pay their groundsmen and the electricity board. It costs £10 or more just to open up a clubhouse for a training night or a large committee meeting. You cannot do it from subscriptions, bar-takings or the Saturday night hop.

Gates *are* important to the big clubs. Spectators will not watch them if their sides cannot match up to the strength of their fixture lists. So the big clubs, who provide the bulk of England's International players, need a constant flow of playing talent. The Exiles seem to be able to arrange this without difficulty. The big clubs cannot any longer. This needs more careful investigation.

I discussed this problem with Alf Wyman, the high priest of Coventry, for whom I have the highest regard when it comes to rugby know-how. Alf told me, with justifiable

Stuart Winship (Wasps and Loughborough scrum-half) is England's leading dropgoaler

pride, that Cov's long-sustained and magnificent strength lies in the fact that there are 26 other clubs, some with as many as five or six sides, in and around Coventry whose main aim is to produce players good enough to play in the Coventry 1st XV. If one of these clubs has one or more players in the Cov. side it arouses great local pride and prestige. I imagine the same thing is well true of other leading Midland and West clubs.

It seems odd that at a time when London clubs are starved of talent coming forward and are producing poor playing results they are surrounded by such clubs as Bristol, Gloucester, Bath, Cheltenham, Moseley, Coventry, Northampton, Leicester, and Bedford, all of whom are doing well, some of them brilliantly.

A few seasons ago I heard John Herbert, a successful Cambridge University, Wasps and England player, now teaching at the famous Treetops school in Victoria, Australia, talking about rugby. "London", said John, "is the Mecca of all ambitious players. The rugby played in London is the best in England." At that time it probably was. But in the Centenary year of the Rugby Union London's rugby, apart from the Exiles, was the poorest I have seen in 32 years; much of it was unworthy of the Extra B on the morning of an International match. It was hard at times to realize there were any coaches operating anywhere.

The reasons are not that complex. For a start young men no longer go to London as I for one did in 1939 with the intention of staying there. It is no longer a Mecca, or a final goal, but a stage in a much longer and far more ambitious journey. Young men, including promising rugby players, go to London for experience and don't stay long. Their firms may only keep them in town for a year or two at the most, and then post them again, or send them abroad. More young men are going abroad on assignments of a business nature than ever before. They include many rugby players, some of real ability and a few of distinction.

London attracts teachers because of the glamour of the capital and the increased London allowances, but they stay on average less than three years before they are on the move again.

"If one has to teach, and it is a vocation", said a London rugby player of note, "then everyone wants to see a bit of London while he is young. But sooner or later he gets married . . . sooner rather than later these days . . . and then the lure of cheaper houses and subsidised accommodation by the education authorities elsewhere will take him away from town. You can live much cheaper in the country or by the seaside somewhere. It is more fun to bring up a family in a village or a market town. Big seaside towns like Blackpool, Brighton, Bournemouth, Torquay and the North Wales coast are much more attractive than London in the long run. And you don't have to go far for good rugby either if you still want it. There might, in fact, be a little, but good, club on your doorstep".

He went on to say something which is at the heart of the London clubs' problem now. "It is, after all, much more fun being a big cheese in a small club than a bit of rind in a big club where you only ever seem to get to know a handful of people".

Young men who are making progress in their careers and hold posts with handles of some kind in their offices, schools, banks and so on do not relish over much the kind of submergence which seems to happen in some London clubs. They talk about "the lack of man-management", whatever that means, "the incorrect utilisation of resources", "the failure to capitalize on talent", "the shortcomings of coaches who can't do everything", "the autocratic allocation of available manpower". They deplore the kind of team selection which results in five wing-forwards playing in one team or a reserve three-quarter being sent a round journey of 80 miles on the day of an International match at Twickenham for a game that was cancelled the previous evening. He neither got a game nor saw the International; the day cost him £5.

The modern young man also hates anonymity, it seems. He is treated as someone of importance in almost every advertisement one reads . . . look at those of the building societies, savings schemes, investments of one kind or another, banks and insurance companies, the jobs advertised in the quality Press, the furniture industry and all consumer goods. Most of them hinge on earlier maturity, earlier marriage and responsibility, including votes at 18.

Whether rugby clubs in the big cities appreciate all this is hard to say. Young men talk about this club and that as being "old men's clubs". What they mean, apparently, is that the club is run by an older generation of whom they do not altogether approve! I cannot really find much evidence to support this in London. There is a very good mixture of generations at all levels, and much harmony. But the clubs *are* big ones which may tend to stifle the ambitions of young men who have had an unfettered life in colleges or universities, stimulated by early success in business, and their personal freedom.

The real cause of the big clubs' troubles lies in inflation. Do clubs realize how much it costs a player to move about the London area when they lightly say "if you want to be considered for the 1st team you must turn up for training on Tuesday and Thursday evenings"? The cost of transport is enormous, not to mention meals, snacks out, sportsgear and laundry. Little wonder that a player of some talent may prefer to stay with a smaller, less fashionable club which only trains one night a week and in practice may not insist on that if circumstances are difficult. A player training two nights a week and travelling long distances for Saturday's game, plus the inevitable Sunday larks, will see little change out of a fiver a week. This, plus the rising cost of flats and accommodation, meals out and the high cost of entertainment of all kinds, makes London very expensive.

"There are far too many tourists in London", complained one player from the Midlands who stayed less than two seasons in town, He was voicing the feeling of many young men from the North, the Midlands and the Commonwealth who feel that London is a crowded, highly expensive "touristy" place these days with all sorts of parking problems, public transport difficulties and endless re-building, which frequently takes a firm to the outskirts of the city or beyond, with further problems of communication and expense.

Players who are teachers, and that includes very many, would prefer one training night a week on Wednesdays, or would like the option of getting fit on their own and reserving one night (Wednesday) for team-training, coaching skills and so on. The reasons are not hard to seek. Teachers find Tuesdays and Thursdays are busy school nights with parents' evenings, school functions and much planning of school work. Wednesday is often a school games day and the one day when they can get away early enough to make sure of a club training session.

Some players, and they include Internationals, tell me that rugby staleness is due to too much training. The best training for rugby is to play the game itself twice a week on Saturdays and Wednesdays at the beginning and latter part of the season, and once a week in mid-season, with a mid-week training night.

Big clubs are already reducing the number of teams fielded to cut costs and are making many economies in other directions, especially in travelling, laundry, postages, telephones, printing, stationery, lighting and heating. They may not be able to afford to open up their grounds and clubhouses for any mid-week training before long; this would only result in the pre-1939 system of getting together only on Saturdays for the most part. Inflation would be the prime cause of that unhappy situation if it arose.

Some of the big clubs are acting as "father figures" with success; Saracens have made Hertfordshire their happy hunting ground and Blackheath are getting back to their old position in Kent. But there is no one easily recognisable "father figure" in Surrey, while Wasps have always maintained they are a London club. Middlesex is a catchment area for any London club, in fact, and officials and players from all clubs live there and work in town.

Apart from competitive rugby and the expected increase in gates to solve some of the pressing financial problems, it seems inevitable that many London clubs need to carry out an urgent major project in public relations if they are to attract players and keep them. Team work off and on the field is essential.

John Williams, British Lions' No. 1 full-back

Rugby's Vigour In The

by Wilfred Woolle

I was born and lived in Colwyn Bay in North Wales and played for the nearest first class club—Sale, which is just on the outskirts of Manchester on the Cheshire side of that great city. In the centre with me when I made the first team was Claude Davey, an outstanding Welsh International and a crash tackler of such power that even my deaf old headmaster, A. J. Costain of Rydal School, could hear the impact of Claude Davey's tackles in my first international game.

I was chosen from *school*, a late developer of 20 who had failed to get into Cambridge that year because of his lack of understanding of Latin. My first game was at Twickenham in 1933. As a North Walian I had not absorbed much of the tradition of Welsh rugby which basically has its heart in the South. I knew but didn't quite appreciate when I was selected, the importance of Twickenham to Wales. I was soon to learn however that in 1910 from the very kick-off by a Welsh forward Gronow, Adrian Stoop of extraordinary incidents saw England recover to win or draw in strange circumstances, not the least of which had been in 1931 when a magnificent penalty kick by Brian Black from the touch-line and half-way, fifty-five yards at least, in the last minute of the match, drew the game 9-all.

I can so well recall that first game being told of the immense noise when playing at Twickenham. The stands over-lap on three sides the edge of the ground and when a crowd of 74,000 is gathered and opens its lungs with a colossal yell, the noise hits the stand and bounces back in a reverberating roar. I recall too the warning that at the end of the two lateral stands which are open at the ends the wind can come driving in at an odd angle and a perfectly good kick for touch may catch the late swirl and swing back into play. All these things I found to be very true and for quarter of an hour at the beginning of that game when I missed the tough thick thighs of Don Burland three times, I was conscious of the unnerving roar of the crowd. In all big games players need a little luck and I was fortunate in that first spell that England only scored once from my errors. Later I was able to adjust my tackling techniques and, taking the powerful West Country centre Burland from the middle to stop him firmly in his tracks.

Ray Hopkins (Maesteg) British Lions No. 2 scrum-half, playing for the Barbarians

had gathered the ball and taken it up field. The English pack had heeled and a try was scored without a Welshman laying his hands on it. That was Wales' first defeat for 11 years by England but when I was selected in 1933 Wales had still not won at Twickenham. They spoke in awe of the Twickenham bogy and it very much seemed as though the English gremlins had personally routed the Welsh on more than one occasion. Games full

The swirl of the wind in that particular game did not catch me out but I was later in some tough hard games with England to find that it did quite frequently affect the course of a kick, and on one occasion when I was playing for Cambridge it took a drop kick past the upright which should have won a game, but was narrowly lost following a great display by Tuppy Owen-Smith the Oxford South African full-back. I saw skilled use made of that wind and those protective stands on occasions by shrewd tactical players and not the least was one of the outstanding Welsh halves Cliff Morgan, who when the Welsh forwards were taking a pounding from England, took the ball up under the shelter of the West Stand where his kick was longer and truer. He kept play down that touch-line for the whole of the second half. Wales won a tactical victory. Apart from winning the 1933 game, the first victory ever by Wales at Twickenham, I did not regard that magnificent English head-quarters as a favourite away ground. On the whole I preferred Murrayfield.

Scottish Teams in my playing days probably had a good deal to do with my liking for Murrayfield. They were well served by Ross Logan at scrum-half and Wilson Shaw at out-half and in the centre Duncan Macrae and Charles Dick. These I thought the four best inside players of any country during my era in the thirties. The tall, hard-running, straight, fast approach of Macrae and Dick presented great tackling problems and I feared them more than any other centres. But a challenge also brings the best out of a player and Scotland were prepared to use the open spaces, run with the ball and attack behind the scrummage. So were Wales. Wales had that incomparable pair Haydn Tanner and Cliff Jones and I played in the centre, for the most part with Claude Davey. We won two very great games at Murrayfeld and only lost a third by a penalty kick in the last minute

In my playing days the Irish match was at Ravenshill in Belfast but we never quite came to terms with the magnificent set of Irish forwards in the thirties with the Beamish brothers, M. Deering, Mike Sayers and Blair Mayne prominent among the superb, heavy-weight Irishmen. Ireland be-

hind the scrummage were inclined to be defensive using the kick as a method of progress and the defensive tackle, lying up on the Welsh back-line and smothering them, as a method of stopping our attacking moves. The games were tremendously hard, very often rough, and frequently fighting broke out, but the moment the game was over the burly Irishmen would arrive in the Welsh dressing room with a crate of Guinness and yarns would be swopped about the punches which had been flying thick and furiously out on the field. However rough the game may be, more often than not when the game is finished players are to be seen laughing about the incidents over a glass of beer.

By the time the Second World War had come and gone and I had finished playing and had become a Press man, and commentator, I had absorbed a great deal of rugby history and tradition. It has never ceased to fascinate me. Why for example does Wales produce an unending stream of brilliant half-backs? A typical Welsh pair of half-backs are rather smaller than taller and lighter than heavier. That is not to say there is not height there and plenty of timber, the good ones have gone around eleven and a half to twelve stone possessing strong limbs and often deep chests. But the Celt is a man of the mountains, dark and tough, quick-moving and quick-thinking and he came, history would have us believe, from the mountain peoples of Europe in the dim and distant past. Maybe he had to be quick-moving and quick-thinking to survive when he was driven from the more lush lands of the English lowlands into the mountains of Wales many, many hundreds of years ago.

Be that as it may, there is a never-ending stream of tough half-backs of whom the great Welsh pair of Haydn Tanner and Cliff Jones

Dauga, brilliant No. 8, feeds the ball to Barrau for France v Wales in Paris, 1971

were incomparable in my day. Cliff Jones, in particular, was a brilliant little side-stepper who could move in and out of trouble like a will-of-the-wisp. Tanner possessed a superb service and a very acute brain which set his play in the right direction. There was another outside-half too, Willie Davies, who played for Swansea, and after he played for Wales went North to become one of the outstanding Rugby League players in his decade. After the war, following in the footsteps of Tanner, came Rex Willis. Perhaps not traditionally Welsh in that he was heavier and moved more along the traditional lines of an English inside-half but, nevertheless, a very great player. His first partner was Billy Cleaver a strong player but he soon found Cliff Morgan, a typical son of the Rhondda, ebullient, fast-

moving, full of life and devil, who lived his Rugby football on and off the field. When Morgan finished there was David Watkins of Newport, a short, stocky, dark and very quick-moving outside-half to step into his shoes. Watkins was tough and a quick thinker and it was a great loss—even near the end of his career—when he decided to move to the professional club Salford in the North. But in no time at all there was stepping into the shoes of the great, the present Welsh half-backs—Gareth Edwards and Barry John. These two are typical Celtic types, dark-haired, quick-thinking, tough and resilient. Indeed Edwards has gone through the gamut of Welsh scrum-half play from being the complete individualist to becoming the perfect team scrum-half with a lovely spinning

49

pass and a perfect sense of when to kick or break. Barry John I rate as one of the great Welsh outside-halves of all time and perhaps the coolest thinker in a crisis. His computer brain decides instantly when it is better to kick for defence or attack, or run the ball along the three-quarter line or even make one of his elusive individual runs. His display against both England and Scotland in 1971 were gems of perfection. He also led the field in England and Wales as a drop-kicker.

The battles are over, the stories begin. Just a few days before I sat down to write this article I was chatting to David Watkins about his experience in Rugby League football which is tough and demanding. Watkins said when he first went to Salford he had to tackle or attempt to tackle a hefty player charging towards him who knocked him flat on his back, where he was very conscious of the fact that he had received a large signing-on fee when joining Salford. Ten minutes later, again he tried to stop one of the big heavy men crashing through. Again he was knocked flying on his back and left floundering in the mud and there was another groan from the crowd. In the midst of this he heard the voice of a wag call out "Hit him with your bloody wallet, Watkins, that's fat enough."

Another current story concerns the Welsh training squad methods. Clive Rowlands is a great believer in the squad system and also in the new mental conditioning of motivation. In the middle of a session he will stop the squad and call out "What are we going to

50

do?" The answering cry comes back "*Win*" and off they go again. A few minutes later he stops them again "What are we going to do?" the answering cry comes back, arms going up in the air, "*Win*". This mental conditioning appears to get the players in the right frame but occasionally to vary the medicine he asks this question and points to a particular player. On this occasion he chose one of the members of the squad who was not in the current side but rather fond of his food. "What are we going to do?" cried Rowlands. And the answering cry came back from the big forward "We are going to eat 'em." The squad session dissolved in laughter.

There are many really good and true stories to be heard in the dressing rooms, or clubhouses where rugby players and their wives, fiancées and girl friends collect. I recall one from playing days. One of my Cambridge colleagues is now a Chief Constable. He was then pack leader of Wales. I regret to say that the Welsh Selectors were not particularly bright at times about the actual game of rugby although they must have been good administrators. We were playing Ireland. During our pre-afternoon match training session which was the only one permitted in my era, a Welsh selector came up to Rees and said "Now Rees, leave a tunnel for the ball to come through." "Right, sir," said Rees, who was always polite to selectors. We lost to Ireland by several points and at the dinner afterwards the very disappointed Welsh selector came up to Arthur Rees and said "Rees, I *am* disappointed. What happened?" "Well, sir," said Rees, "we left a tunnel just like you said, sir, but the trouble was the whole bloody Irish pack came through it!"

It is the custom of many rugby followers of their country to travel to the International matches on Friday evening, returning on Sunday and from Wales innumerable clubs all year save, and travel by excursions to make a weekend of real enjoyment. The result is that the night before the game the hotels are full of rugby followers. Friday is one big debate on prospects, Saturday is the post-mortem. Much of the discussion fortunately goes unrecorded but one incident did live. It was the season 1950–1 when Wales had taken twenty-three points off England in Swansea after winning the Triple Crown the previous year. They travelled to Murrayfield to play Scotland full of confidence and every supporter who went with them, and there were nearly 20,000, decided it was merely a matter of how many points Wales could win by. It is on record that one reporter, quite a respectable journalist, had a bet in the Press Club on the Friday night that Wales would be the first country to win by 50 points. The following day came the biggest upset of all time. Wales lost by 19 points. He must surely be the only journalist ever to be 69 points out in a forecast of an International game. We cannot all win, can we?

EXOTIC CLUBS QUIZ I

Many clubs playing in England have exotic names. Here are ten of them, but in fact two are fictitious. Can you name these two?
1. B.O.A.C. Speedbird 2. Brookhurst Igranic
3. Barker's Butts 4. London Fire Brigade
5. Leeds Telephones 6. Bolton Toc H
7. Hong Kong and Shanghai Bank
8. Zurich Insurance
9. Kidderminster Carolians 10. Choristers

Solution on Page 93

Dear Uncle

Another mixed postbag from readers, ranging from mysterious blondes to tea-room etiquette. Send your rugby problems to Uncle Jack c/o "World of Rugby", St Giles' House, 49/50, Poland Street, London W1A 2LG. Confidences will be respected at all times, unless the security of the State is involved.

Strange Blonde

In our club, which is not regarded as first-class, or indeed any class, we are much troubled by a mysterious blonde who contrives to appear in the clubhouse every

"How long is it likely to last, Guv? Kick-off is at three o'clock."

Saturday evening, giving the impression most successfully that she is the close friend of a player (never named) or one of the opposition. What can we do about her? Our committee seem nonplussed.

"Worried" (Lower Bassenthwaite)

First ascertain if she *is* known to any member. Circulate a photo taken without her knowledge with a brief description. If you draw a blank then the club chairman or secretary should approach her boldly, waving a piece of paper and saying that he would like to propose her as a lady member, even if you do not at the moment have them. Ensure he has a witness, who will act as seconder if needed. If the lady is genuine she will readily wish to join the club and pay a subscription. You can then put her on tea-room duty at once as every club needs help of this kind. But if she turns pale and flees you know she is a phoney, and probably had ulterior motives. You will then never see her again.

Nowty Skipper

Our skipper is not very popular, probably because he was only elected on the casting vote of the President, whom we suspect to be his insurance broker. In the dressing-room he is very silent (the skipper I mean) and tends to take a long time doing up his boots when he ought to be discussing tactics. He is very nowty after the game, even when we win. How can we improve things, while hoping he will find an interest elsewhere to take his mind away from rugby?

Name and club withheld (Llareggub)
This is a fairly common problem, my dears, and you may have to live with it to the end of the season, when you should ensure the President is not able to place a casting vote in favour of his client. You must ensure that at the annual meeting an urgent phone call is received for him shortly before the subject is voted upon. For example, vandals believed to be at work on his car, or a flooded river threatening the safety of his office, or a similar catastrophe. By the time he is back on the dais, with the phone call happily proving to be that of someone else with the same name, the vote will have been taken and your nominee will be in. There are times when we must be ruthless in rugby and this is one of them. The game is bigger than the players. A nowty skipper is not worth his weight in anything. Have patience.

Dogs on Pitch

Our club's fixture with London Welsh is shortly upon us and we fear the worst, as ever. As you know they have two brilliant 1st XV's and lull the opposition into believing they are playing reserves on the days of International matches. Thus they beat Bedford 29–3 on the same day they provided Wales with six players in the 19–18 defeat of Scotland at Murrayfield, and also allowed two more stars to go to Llanelli for a wedding. How *can* we hope to beat them? The situation is nightmarish, with the Red Devils of the Old Deer Park upon us.

*The Hon. Aubrey Thornton-Cleveleys
(Harlequins)*
This problem is a daily one for any club anywhere. But take heart. It is only two years or less since Wasps *thrashed* London Welsh 19–6 plus two perfectly good tries

disallowed under the posts. The victory was achieved with the use of carefully-trained dogs. Whenever London Welsh threatened danger a yellow Labrador dog was released from that side of the pitch, causing a trail of havoc among the Welsh players as it raced madly about, scenting aniseed laid in strategic places well before the game. By the time order had been restored the Wasps line was in no danger. Later one or more dogs were released on the opposite side of the pitch and the same thing happened again. But one of them was a bitch, and in no time there were five more unscheduled dogs chasing her. The referee blew his final whistle seven minutes early but he said it was for bad light. Some might call this gamesmanship.

Water Bottle "Tainted with Rum"

Do you think that referees should check the contents of the first-aid men's water-bottles before a game? The reason we ask this arises from last Saturday's defeat at the hands of the Old Merchant Seamen. The O.M.S. were experts at collapsing the scrum on our put-in,

"Why me, Sir?"

and on more than one occasion our poor old hooker was nearly asphyxiated under the weight of too, too solid flesh. Every time their first-aid man rushed on and slapped his cheeks, followed by a water-bottle forced down his throat. There was nothing we could do about it as we had no first-aid man of our own. Our hooker's powers declined rapidly and in the last quarter, when he failed to get the ball even once, he was talking to himself and the props said he reeked of rum. We now think the water-bottle was tainted and we are thinking of cancelling the fixture. Is there no honour left in rugby?

Jeremy Shorthouse (Hon. Sec.,
Old Billpostians)

"Plays anywhere—most useful"

To answer your last question first, opinion differs. We do not think referees should be asked to examine, sniff or taste the contents of water-bottles in the first-aid department before a game. They have too much to do already. In any case the bottles are always filthy. It is up to you and your fellow

Billpostians to be alive to all emergencies. You must rush on the field and attend to your own wounded when the occasion arises,

"Why do the Harlequins always want to be in the front?"

even if you have nothing with which to sustain the victim; it should not be too difficult to arrange for someone to carry a bottle of pure water about with him drawn from his own undefiled tap at home, or well. After all, one would expect Old Merchant Seamen to carry rum with them on most occasions. Imagine what would happen if you played a team of professional cyclists! They carry water-bottles filled with honey, glucose, Ovaltine, maple syrup and the most revolting milky rice-pudding. Your complaint is a trivial one. Have more sense.

Meet you next time in World of Rugby *with another batch of readers' questions and replies of wide general interest. Even though Uncle Jack can't answer every query personally, much as he'd love to do so, he really does read every letter and finds them tremendously interesting. Thank you again for writing.—Editor.*

Goal Kicking Competitions Reveal Talent

by Jack Cox

Goals, and the players who kick them, win matches and are the basis of club records over the years; after all, this means an extra two or three points a time. Competitions are fun, finding talent and raising money.

However much they are decried at times, goals do win more matches than tries. If records are the yardstick of club seniority, and they are the making of fixture lists, then goals count enormously. No big club can afford to be without a competent goal-kicker, preferably two. An analysis of the records of all leading Welsh and English clubs over the years shows that goals kicked at the moment when they were wanted most gave these clubs their outstanding records and playing success. Fixture lists, in fact, always depend far more on goals than tries.

To prove the point make a note of the current games that your own club could have won with accurate goalkicking. Compare the season's results of the club, as published in the national newspapers on Tuesday mornings, with your own knowledge of what it could be with better kicking. Think of what Sam Doble's kicking means to Moseley or Bob Hiller's to Harlequins. When you are playing against tough opposition there is nothing like the morale-booster of a few extra points produced by your place-kicker, adding two points to a well-earned try, or putting over a 50-yard penalty at a vital stage of the game.

We often forget that goals were all-important in the early formative years of rugby, so much so that a player had to touch the ball down over his opponent's line in order to have a try at kicking a goal! That is where the word "try" comes from. Kicking a ball between the posts and under the bar, as in association football, was considered too easy. They lashed a couple of posts on the uprights, only a few feet high, incidentally, as you can see in all the early drawings and photos. Then they started to kick rugby goals over the bar and between the lashed poles because it was more difficult. The side poles became higher and higher as disputes arose about kicks that sailed over in the region of the uprights. Eventually posts were high enough for everybody.

Think for a moment of England's shocking goal-kicking at Cardiff on January 16, 1970. Some 17 points were frittered away by appalling kicking by Rossborough and Larter. What a difference it might have made if some kicks had gone over at the vital stage when Wales were getting their tails up! How much better the final score would have looked if it had been, 22–16 in Wales' favour instead of 22–6. One would have thought that England would have learned their lesson long ago.

In my opinion a place-kicker, preferably a

well-made prop, lock or No. 8, with a kick like a mule which can be cultivated with regular practice, is always worth his place in a side, even if in later years he only pads from scrum to scrum or line-out to line-out. So long as he is really doing his job in the tight, staying as near to the ball as possible at all times, and kicking his goals, especially when they count most, he is worth his weight in gold! All 17 stones of it.

Practice is all-important to anyone with the basic skill and talent, no matter what his style may be. Twenty minutes a day on every day except match-days is one scheme which has been extremely successful in the past for kickers who could persuade a friend or brother to go out with them during lunch hours in all weathers on any kind of pitch available . . . a soccer or hockey pitch, a public park or common, a school playing-field, or best of all naturally, a club pitch.

Twenty to thirty minutes a day of dedicated practice is better than the occasional hour on a Sunday afternoon or evening at the begin-ning or end of the season. It does need devotion to the job, the kind of dedication that a top player of any game needs to give to his craft and skill.

Then there is drop-kicking, one of the great arts of rugby which can definitely be learned by anyone with kicking talent. There is a peculiar delight in playing in a team which has a good drop-goaler in it. Harry Bowcott, a distinguished Welsh International stand-off, now chairman of the Welsh selectors, inspired any team he played in with the rich quality of his drop-kicking. For several seasons he was the keystone of the Wasps' side in which I played. Having laboured fiercely and successfully to get the ball in a tight scrum it was a wonderful feeling to rise and find to one's delight that

Bob Hiller's perfect place-kicking technique

Harry Bowcott had either dropped a goal from near half-way or had almost done so. It always demoralised the opposition. On the other hand there is nothing more disheartening for a forward than to get the ball cleanly only to find incompetence elsewhere has driven the pack 25 yards back instead of forward.

There are some fine drop-goalers about just now. Watch John Moroney (London Irish), Barry John (Cardiff) and Stuart Winship (Wasps), for instance, who between them had notched 30 little more than half-way through the 1970–1 season. Half-backs or wing-forwards seem to get the spot opportunities. Again, practice is all-important.

There may well be talent in your own club that you hardly suspect, which is the real purpose of this article. I suggest that you run an annual Goal-kicking Competition to find the talent, and once it is found to develop it and use it to the full. The best time for such a competition is at the beginning of the season, perhaps towards the end of September when the early preliminaries are over and the season is just getting under way. But it can be held at any time if that is not convenient.

Such competitions are not new but they have tended to be neglected. As a student too long ago I well remember the Dean Cup at Manchester University which was set up for this very purpose. When I enquired what had happened to the competition some 25 years later the cup was found, black with age, in a derelict cupboard in the Union, put away for the war, and long forgotten.

A better idea, which has been adopted by Surrey University in recent years, is to have a pot for each annual tournament to be won

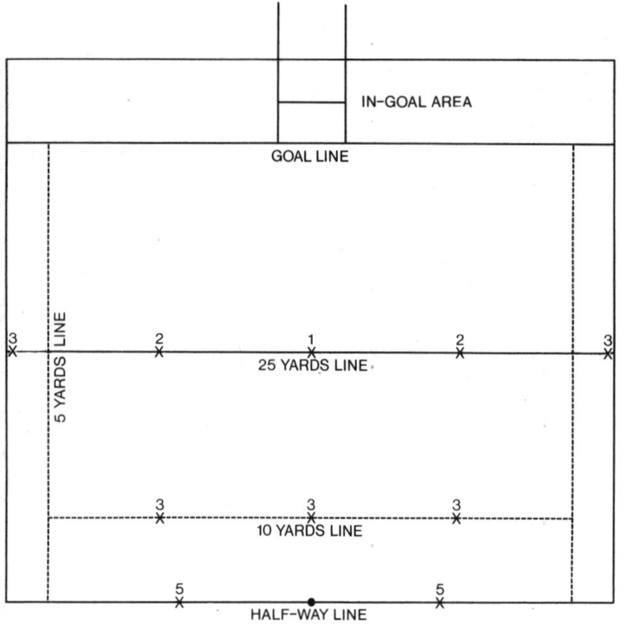

This plan of one half of the field of play shows the ten suggested points for kicks at goal and the number of points allocated to each, by the author, so that there is a maximum of 30 points

If there is a large entry, as usually happens, preliminary rounds need to be settled first so that on the final day a tournament can last about three hours.

Two methods of running the competition have been tried but the best is the simplest. Each kicker has a shot at ten goals in all, and for the purposes of the competition it is best to kick with the wind and to take all the kicks at one goal. Kicking with the wind does give confidence to players who normally never kick at all. Seven of the ten kicks must be placed goals, as in conversions or penalties, and three must be dropped. The kicker has the option of deciding which of his ten goals shall be dropped. It is still not generally realized by players that a try can be converted with a dropped goal (See Law 13, paragraph 1). On a blustery day when the ground is hard and the ball can't be placed easily a drop is always a good bet.

The first five kicks are all taken on one line at a range of 25 to 30 yards, one of which must be in front of the posts. The remaining kicks are on the left and right respectively, one kick in each case being half-way between the posts and the touch-line. The two outer kicks are both on the touchline, as if a wing had scored a try in the corner and a conversion was being taken.

The next three kicks are from the 10 yards line at a range of about 40 to 45 yards. One kick should be dead centre in front of the posts, the other two being on either side of the field half-way between the posts and the touch-line. These kicks are all typical positions of penalties in any game, and are good ones for dropping.

The final two kicks are long-distance efforts from half-way, but not the centre. One should be on the left and the other on the right, say about half-way between the

outright. They had a vice-president willing and able to provide an inscribed tankard for the winners. It makes a very good day's sport and a social gathering not to be missed. On every occasion Surrey University have found new goal-kicking talent which they have then exploited to their advantage during the season.

In 1970–1 season the winner was a player they didn't even know they had! He happened to be a research student at Surrey for one year on release from the Royal Navy in Scotland. He put his name down, kicked his competition goals, walked off with the trophy and endeared himself to the side for a season. Excellent.

Any student in residence can enter the Surrey competition, which is held on a Sunday early in the academic year on their magnificent new playing fields at Guildford.

centre of the field and the touch-line.

Every successful kick earns points on the following ratio. The first five kicks: 1 point for the kick under the posts, 2 each for the two inner kicks on either side of the field midway between the posts and touch-line, and 3 points for each of the touch-line conversions. Maximum for these 5 kicks is thus 11 points.

The next three kicks are assessed at 3 points each, and the two from half-way at 5 points each, making a grand possible total of 30 points. The winner of the inscribed tankard is the player with the highest number of points on the final day.

If the goal-kicking competition ends in a tie then the players at that stage must have a play-off. This can be a "sudden death" effort of just one goal-kick to be taken by each player from any point determined by the Master of Ceremonies, but it is more fun to have a play-off of a further three or five goals kicked into the wind at the other end of the pitch. If there is no wind (that rugby should see such a day!) the same posts are used. In play-offs every goal counts one point only which is sure to give a final close result.

The greatest number of points scored by any one player in the three Surrey tournaments up to 1971 has been 23. The highest number of points in any tournament I have ever organized on these lines has been 28. The average is about 20 to 23. I have not yet known a single goal-kicking competition which did not produce unsuspected talent which was later exploited for the benefit of the club. It also enables a club to assess a new player more expertly since the average new player tends to be very diffident about his skills and rarely gives a true picture of what he can or cannot do.

It is much better if a kicker does not take all his ten kicks at once. The first five kicks on the 25–30 yard range can be kicked one after the other, the players taking part in alphabetical order to save time. Several balls should be used, and not more than one new ball. When the first range of kicks is finished and points noted by the scorers, the second range of three kicks is taken the same way, and finally the third. There can be a tea interval if you have enough entries to ensure a grand slam finish for the big kicks of the day.

Another idea if you are getting a very close finish is to award a half-point for any kick which hits a post. In the early days of rugby "posters" were regarded as very important features of the game; in the event of a tie in the number of goals scored, a match could be *drawn in favour of one side or the other*, the favoured side being the one with the biggest tally of posters. Kicks which failed to go over the bar but hit a post always have an honourable standing in the game. It is surprising in a goal-kicking competition how many kicks do hit the posts. In the 1970–1 Surrey University tournament there were 11 on the final day. A half-point for posters could eliminate any play-offs probably.

Finally, you will make money. It is a pleasant social occasion for the club and their friends and families. Players are allowed to kick in normal kit or track suits but not in any old garb. Make an occasion of it and have a decent presentation in the bar afterwards. Soon it could become an annual institution in late September. It might even be possible to let the winner enter a County competition on similar lines. It would be of value to find out the best goal-kickers in any County. They may well never have been contemplated for County honours.

Goals That Counted

by Rex Alston

It is exciting to recall the famous occasions when goal-kicking decided the issue, the most recent being the Calcutta Cup match of 1971, when Scotland beat England 16–15 at Twickenham in a memorable victory. In these days of penalty goals galore and the occasional drop goal, I have cast my mind back to matches which have been decided by goal kicking—conversion, drop or penalty.

I remember an extraordinary match against Wales at Twickenham on a blustery January day in 1923. I was standing on the mound behind the north goal posts—the present stand had not then been built. England kicked off into the gale and the ball soared into the air, eluded all Welsh hands, and was swept into the arms of England's wing-forward, H. L. Price, following up hard. He ran straight on and punted towards goal. The ball ballooned up, was again swept back by the wind and clear of clutching Welsh hands, and there was Price snatching it up a second time to score a sensational try at the posts before anyone had taken breath. No one else on either side had touched the ball. So great was the shock that the unfortunate G. S. Conway, front-row forward and experienced goal-kicker, fluffed the easy conversion.

The game then settled down into the usual

tough, forward struggle, and when Wales equalised, with an unconverted try, it looked as though that missed conversion would cost England the match. However, with the wind behind them in the second half, England should have clinched matters, but the Welsh somehow kept them out and the English backs were not in form. Then suddenly in mid-field, that most artistic of English centres, L. J. Corbett, always full of tricks, picked up a loose ball in broken play and flicked it between his legs backwards to his wing, A. M. Smallwood. Perhaps this was a rehearsed gambit, for Smallwood, as though prepared for such an unorthodox manoeuvre, caught the ball, and from half-way out dropped a superb long-range goal. That finally snuffed out Welsh resistance and England won 7–3. Who shall say that such a kick on such a day was not worth four points?

The presence of an expert goal-kicker had saved England the season before against France. In a frenzied first half, the French pack were twice penalised and H. L. V. Day, playing on the left-wing, kicked two goals. In the second half, the French scored a goal and two tries and, leading 11–6, looked all set to record their first-ever win at Twickenham. The English pack then made a supreme effort and A. T. Voyce rounded off a forward rush with a try. So all depended on the goal-kick, and Harold Day—legend had it that he was playing in borrowed boots—saved the day to give England a draw at 11-all.

Now let's move to Scotland for the opening of Murrayfield in 1925, with the Calcutta Cup at stake. Scotland's famous Oxford three-quarter line—I. S. Smith, G. P. S. McPherson, and the two "Colonial" Scots, G. G. Aitken and A. C. Wallace—were faced

Grahame Hodgson, Neath's deadly goal-kicker

with an ageing though talented England, who led 8–5 at half-time. Then Wakefield scored for England, but the Scots charged the easy kick down—11–5 to England. Towards the end Wallace just managed to scramble over in the corner and wing forward A. C. Gillies kicked a marvellous goal from touch—11–10. With time running short, H. Waddle, at stand-off for Scotland, now began scheming with scrum-half J. B. Nelson for a drop goal. The first attempt failed, but the pack gave him another chance and over the ball went—11–14 to Scotland. The last stages were especially hectic as the weary English made a last effort, and we are told that Corbett, with the line open a yard or two away, "staggered and fell from exhaustion". Obviously they didn't train in those days like the moderns. So Scotland opened their magnificent new ground with a memorable victory and went on to win the championship.

A different sort of drop goal clinched a South African victory at Twickenham in 1932. Again, I was stationed behind the northern goalposts, and had a close-up of the two crucial incidents which decided the game. As usual, it was controlled by a heavy South African pack, supported by a shrewd tactical kicker at stand-off in B. L. Osler. But the English defence was heroic, and the South African backs, on the few occasions when Osler let them have the ball, achieved nothing. The result centred round the play of England's new full-back, R. J. Barr. He managed to half stop a fly-kick by a South African forward which went on over the line. Barr turned to try and touch down, slipped, and two South African forwards beat him to it as he made a despairing effort to get his hand on the ball. Surprisingly the try was not converted.

Shortly afterwards South Africa were penal-

ised near the English posts. Barr, normally a reliable kicker, failed to find a long touch, and G. Brand, South Africa's elegant full-back, fielded the ball and dropped a marvellous left-footed long-range goal which curled high between the uprights. Barr's cup of misery was full, but to his credit he made no more mistakes, and though England lost 7–0, his all-round play was so sound that he won two more caps in the next two matches.

Another match-winning drop came off at Twickenham against Wales in 1937. Again it was a full-back failure to find touch which gave H. S. Sever his moment of inspiration, and again it was an English left-wing who kicked the goal. I did not see it myself, but I gather that Vivian Jenkins' kick to touch was partially fielded by one of the England forwards, Robin Prescott, now Secretary of the Rugby Union. The ball went behind him over his shoulder and Hal Sever, noted more for his bull-like rushes for the line than for his kicking ability, pounced on it and from an acute angle, scored England's four points. Later, Wilfred Wooller scored a try for Wales but Jenkins was unable to convert, so England won by the unusual score 4–3.

In all the dozens of international matches which I have seen since 1945, perhaps the most remarkable upset of form was at Murrayfield in 1951. Wales, full of Lions' backs who had taken New Zealand by storm the previous summer, and had run up 23 points against England a fortnight before, were confronted by a youthful and inexperienced Scottish team. But those famous Welshmen—Ken Jones, Jack Matthews, Lewis Jones, Malcolm Thomas, Glyn Davies and Rex Willis, were knocked off their game, and with 20 minutes left Scotland were

Sam Doble (Moseley), leading England points scorer

leading by a penalty goal to nil. Then Gerwyn Williams, who had played an immaculate game at full-back, failed to find touch from near his own posts and Peter Kininmonth, the Scottish captain, standing on the touchline near the 25, caught the ball and dropped a soaring goal. This so flabbergasted the Welsh and so inspired the Scots that they overran their dispirited opponents and won 19–0. If ever a kick turned a match, that Kininmonth "special" did.

Though not so abundant as in these days, penalty goals have won important matches in the past. When Wales paid their first post-war visit to Paris, France was in the middle of a mini-heatwave. The ground was bone-hard and the sun poured down on shirt-sleeved spectators—conditions which should have suited the French. The weather was belatedly making up for the big freeze which had so disrupted the rugby programme earlier in 1947.

The match was chiefly memorable for one decisive incident. The Welsh backs included Ken Jones and Bleddyn Williams, and had W. B. Cleaver and Haydn Tanner at half-back, but were well-held. The crucial penalty was awarded in the second half just inside the Welsh half and in mid-field. I remember Bill Tamplin, the big second-row forward, having a job to make a mark on the hard ground. But at last the ball was set up for him, and taking a long run he gave it a monumental thump which sent it far and low and just over the bar. A poor way to win a match, maybe, but it helped Wales to share the first post-war championship with England.

Conditions were reversed three years later when Ireland were the visitors. Paris was gripped by a bitter frost, and despite straw on the ground, it was doubtful if the match could be played. However, the players decided to risk it and fortunately no one was seriously hurt. In a hard and unskillful game, liberally strewn with penalties, three incidents stand out in my mind. Lauga, the French stand-off half and expert drop kick, had three early shots at goal. The first failed, the second went over the bar just after the referee had blown for a previous off-side, and the crowd, not understanding what was wrong, made a rare hullabaloo when Jean Prat's penalty failed. Lauga's third attempt was successful, and so the score remained 3–0 till the closing minutes.

Then Arcalis, a diminutive but exciting full-back, essayed a long drop from far out near touch and the ball rebounded off the far upright. Ireland had a last chance to save the game with only a minute to go when they were awarded a penalty in the French 25. It was not a difficult kick, and because Ireland's regular kickers had all previously failed, Karl Mullen, the Irish captain, took a chance and threw the ball to Burges, the new scrum-half playing his first match. Despite the jeers of the crowd, he duly slotted the all-important goal and ensured a 3–3 draw.

Another first cap who won a match with the final kick was T. Gray, Scotland's full-back against England at Murrayfield in 1950. In appalling conditions of rain and wind, both sides played exciting rugby and England 8–3 down at half-time, made a strong recovery to lead 11–8 with a few minutes left. Scotland, who had scarcely deserved to be behind, then rushed the ball to near the English line where, after a hectic *mêlée*, they scored through Sloan. Gray, who had earlier converted a try, took the decisive kick for victory. It was no more difficult than Burges's in Paris, and, of course, he had the crowd with him, but he had to contend with a heavy, greasy ball. His nerve did not fail, and the ball went safely over to give Scotland a fine win, 13–11.

Reverting to drop-kicks, when representative rugby started again after World War II, no regular programme was arranged. Scotland came to Twickenham with a big reputation won by victories over the touring Kiwis, Wales and Ireland. They built up a lead of eight points, but England counter-attacked in the second half and levelled the score with a fine threequarter try converted from touch by Jack Heaton, who had also kicked a penalty. With the score 8–all, England continued to press till, suddenly, Keith Scott, playing in the centre, seized on a loose ball in the Scots 25 and dropped a snap goal to give England victory—12–8.

In a return game at Murrayfield in April, Scotland had ample revenge with a 27–nil win, thus proving themselves the best side in the famous "Victory Internationals".

Drop-kicks, reduced in value to three points in 1948–9, played an important part in a county match at Manchester between Lancashire and Yorkshire, which was decisive for the group leadership, and useful to the England selectors, because the halves, M. Regan and G. Rimmer for Lancashire and E. M. P. Hardy and D. W. Shuttleworth for Yorkshire, had been picked in opposition for the second England trial on the following Saturday. The game, easily won by Yorkshire, 22–5, finished in darkness so that it was virtually impossible to follow the ball, but earlier Hardy had dropped two goals, *one with each foot*, which may be without precedent, certainly in the same match.

Kicking played a decisive part in a surprise Irish victory over England in Dublin in 1961. Andy Mulligan, the Irish scrum-half, had gone down with measles, and the selectors, with a typically charming disregard for more

obvious candidates, chose in his place J. W. Moffett, a name virtually unknown to the English party, who had played most of his rugby at wing-forward or in the centre. A burly, fair-haired man, he was to be the key figure as a place-kicker. Not only did he play supremely well as a scrum-half, but he kicked two penalties in the first half and then converted a try to give Ireland an 11–0 lead. England rallied and scored a goal and a try, the latter by D. P. Rogers in his first international—but Moffett of Ballymena, whose eight points won the match for Ireland, was the toast of Dublin that night.

The supreme example of goals that won matches was the Test in New Zealand in 1959 which Don Clarke won by kicking six penalties when the Lions had crossed the New Zealand line four times, yet lost 18–17! Of more recent memory were Hiller's two huge drops within two minutes of each other which won England a scarcely deserved victory by nine points to three over Ireland at Twickenham in 1970, and Peter Brown's nonchalant conversion which won the Calcutta Cup for Scotland in 1971, their first win (16–15) at Twickenham for 33 years!

Bob Hiller kicks a penalty for England v Scotland, 1971 ▶

EXOTIC CLUBS QUIZ II

Many clubs playing in England have exotic names. Here are ten more of them, but in fact two are fictitious. Can you name these two?

1. Battersea Ironsides
2. Somerset and Bath Constabulary
3. International Synthetic Rubber 4. Sun
5. Great Western Railway
6. Buile Hill All Stars
7. Northampton Old Scouts
8. Yorkshire Copper Works
9. Skipton Tigers 10. Inland Revenue

Solution on Page 93

The Scarlet Magic of Llanelli

by Ron Griffiths

Llanelli, a giant among rugby clubs, have produced well over 100 International players and celebrate their own Centenary in 1972. If Liverpool is the capital city of soccer, then Llanelli must surely be the capital of rugby.

This Carmarthenshire town has an unique devotion to the game demonstrated week in, week out as the faithful flock like pilgrims to Mecca to Stradey Park.

Stradey . . . a name as famous to rugby men as Cardiff Arms Park, Twickenham or Murrayfield. There you will find the true rugby spirit and a real sense of belonging to the game. For rugby is much more than just a game in Llanelli, it's a way of life.

The deeds of the team in their famous scarlet jerseys command so much attention it's often been said they get more spectators at a training session than some clubs do at matches. That sort of fanatical interest must rival even New Zealand. It also explains why so many great players, among them well over 100 internationals, consider it a privilege to play for a club.

Now Llanelli is approaching its centenary and you can rely on their celebrations being the biggest, and the most ambitious. As one official put it to me, "This is Llanelli, isn't it? We never do things by half-measures here".

He's right, of course. Why, the club once went into mourning for six months when one of the early stalwarts, a certain Arthur Buchanan, accidentally shot himself while wild-fowling on the marshes to the west of the town!

Buchanan had taken over the reins of the club established much earlier, in 1872, in

fact, by a young man named John D. Rogers, who later became a prominent South Wales industrialist. Rogers, who had learned the game at its birthplace, Rugby School, brought together a group of young athletes and taught them the rudiments of the game on an undeveloped open space in the town centre.

His action, needless to say, wasn't universally approved. It incurred severe criticism from the Nonconformist core in the pulpits and the weekly newspapers. They demanded the banning of "this ruffianly game".

But Rogers, backed by two ardent supporters, Fred L. Margrave and W. Buckley Roderick—both to play for Wales later—not only rode the storm but destroyed the prejudices by their exemplary conduct on and off the field.

Soon the town's attitude to rugby did a remarkable about-turn. Even the Press, so critical previously, were now ready to offer praise. The "ruffianly game" became this "manly game", and one editor urged the young to shun the taverns and "follow the lead of these fine football fellows".

This was the turning point. Rugby was not only socially accepted—it was now a rallying point as well. By 1875 Rogers' sporting flock was ready to spread its wings and when a club named Cambria was formed at Swansea he immediately launched his team into the inter-town rivalry that still exists.

In 1880–81, Llanelli, under the captaincy of Fred L. Margrave, were one of the clubs represented at the formation meeting of the Welsh Rugby Union. By now Llanelli's fame was becoming well known. When the South Wales Challenge Cup was instituted they were in five finals between 1881 and 1887, twice winning the trophy.

◀ *Phil Bennett prefers water at half-time!*

The club's first caps were D. Harry Bowen, Arthur Cattell and J. H. Judson in 1883. They could have had earlier representatives but Roderick and Margrave declined to play because the internationals for which they were chosen clashed with important club cup-ties!

Since then Llanelli's contribution to Wales has been considerable. They had eight players in the Welsh XV against Ireland in 1928 and six in the side which beat Australia in 1958. Once they had 10 caps in their club side at the same time.

The move to Stradey Park came in 1879 when the squire of Stradey, Mr. C. W. Lewis, became the President. The club colours were then blue, later changed to rose and primrose hoops and then, in 1881–82, the now famous scarlet jersey was approved.

Perhaps Llanelli's greatest season was 1895–96 when invincibility eluded them by one of the cruellest caprices of fate. They had swept all before them when they set off on a short tour to Gloucester and Leicester.

Against Gloucester, with Llanelli trailing by two points late in the game, a wing crashed over in the corner. The Llanelli touch-judge was so excited he waved his flag—and the referee rightly blew for a line-out on the line. The record was lost.

Australia were beaten for the first time in 1908 and since then Llanelli have had two epic matches with the Springboks separated by 58 years. In 1912 they lost by a point and again in 1970 in one of the most exciting matches of the tour.

After World War I Llanelli continued to grow in stature. The pack had the beneficent, if not docile, guidance of such forwards as the Rev. W. T. Havard (later to become Bishop of St. David's) and the Rev. J. G. Stephens.

Chris Wardlow (Northampton) moves in to tackle W. Lewis (Llanelli) at Franklin's Gardens

Delme Thomas wins a line-out for Wales v Ireland at Cardiff, 1971

Then came Ivor Jones, a former president of the Welsh Rugby Union, who brought artistry and craft to the back-row for club, country and the British Lions. He and another Llanelli product of more recent vintage, lock Rhys Williams, are still considered by New Zealanders among the finest British forwards ever to tour in their country.

After Ivor Jones there was Archie Skym, the only forward ever to be picked by Wales in all three rows of the scrum. Next the thirties and the seam of Llanelli talent remained as rich as ever . . . forwards like Jim Lang and Bryn Evans, threequarters Bill Clement, now the Welsh RU secretary, and Elvet Jones, a former Llanelli chairman. Both toured South Africa with the 1938 British Lions.

The players continued to come off the Llanelli production line after World War II. Terry Davies and Terry Price, two gifted full-backs, centres Cyril Davies, Ken Jones, Lewis Jones, half-backs Carwyn James, the present club coach, Barry John, now at Cardiff, and Phil Bennett, forwards Norman Gale, Delme Thomas and Stuart Gallacher . . . the list is unending.

Llanelli made rugby history when they became the first British club side to play in Moscow in 1957. The occasion was the World Youth Festival of Sport and Llanelli lost to Rumania in a replay of the final.

If that was an important landmark in the club's history, perhaps an even more important one was some years earlier when Stradey Park was purchased. Once the deal had been completed, under the successive chairmanship of Dr. E. Noel Rees, Handel Rogers, now a WRU district member, Elvet Jones and Peter Rees, there began an ambitious development programme that is still in progress.

New stands, a dining-room and a changing block have been built, new terracing constructed, car parks laid out to accommodate over 1,000 cars, and floodlighting installed. All this underlines the tremendous drive that exists within this great club.

Delme Thomas (British Lions) in form for England & Wales v Scotland & Ireland, 1970–71

Saracens' Steady Climb

by Micheal Eaton

Founded by old boys of St. Marylebone Grammer School in 1876 Saracens' progress in recent seasons can be traced directly to coaching skills.

Saracens are pacing themselves so nicely that they may well reach their peak in their centenary year of 1976. Since 1945 Saracens' stature in the rugby world has grown steadily with improved fixtures being matched by improved results.

Proof of their continuing development? The fixture list provides the answer with Neath, Newbridge and Northampton—a most formidable trio—appearing for the first time on a regular basis. Blackheath are the prize addition in season 1971–2 and that will leave Saracens almost satisfied.

Yes, almost satisfied. Coventry, Moseley, Newport, Harlequins and Cardiff still remain to be cajoled into providing opposition! In fact Moseley have agreed to a meeting between the second teams, and Saracens are realistic enough to see that too many new, difficult matches could be harmful.

However, the strength of opposition has improved immeasurably since 1945 with Bath, London Irish, Richmond, Ebbw Vale, Gloucester, Bedford and Leicester among the pick of the newcomers. One of the highlights for Saracens in 1969 was their defeat of Bedford when the latter were England's top side with only one defeat, and feared throughout the country. Last season they thrashed a strong Ebbw Vale 26–10.

Saracens were the brain-child of former pupils of St. Marylebone Grammar School in London. They founded the club in 1876 when the vogue was to give exotic names to clubs and ignore the mundane town or district association. Founded in 1876 at Hampstead, Saracens therefore grew up alongside Wasps, Barbarians and Harlequins all founded in Hampstead in the previous decade. Also founded in Hampstead in 1879, three years after Saracens, was Rosslyn Park.

The eastern influence in the name was perhaps to blame for the club being nomadic as well. They have settled briefly at several grounds in North London and before they arrived at Winchmore Hill between the two World Wars the club had nose-dived from a position of some eminence.

At Winchmore Hill the situation improved and eventually the club had grounds leased to them from the Council to match the splendid new pavilion opened at Southgate in 1939. No sooner had the grand opening been completed than the Army took it over and the club did not reoccupy it again until 1946. Since then Saracens have flourished. The climax to date was the 1967-68 season when it was records all the way. They had a record number of 27 wins since the war and scored a record number of points in a season with 616, a total exceeded last season.

Naturally, the accent throughout was on

Keith McIntyre (Wasps and Bart's Hospital) playing for Middlesex v Eastern Counties

attacking rugby and plenty of back play. Phil Clark and Tony Janaway, the two first-choice wingers, had a tremendous duel for the honour of scoring the most tries and Clark, a Sussex cap, finally edged out Janaway, an Eastern Counties player. The tally was 25–22.

At a representative level the Saracens were puffing out their chests with pride. Seventeen players won county honours—a club record—and for George Sherriff, Roger Weaver and Mike Alder this meant a share in Middlesex's County championship final triumph over Warwickshire.

Alder, a gifted but ultra-conscientious stand-off, earned an England trial, while Sherriff was capped against the New Zealand All Blacks. To climax a memorable season, Saracens reached the semi-finals of the Middlesex Sevens at Twickenham before losing to Richmond, the beaten finalists.

Saracens have achieved their successes without any recognised source of talent. No local schools are natural nurseries and Oxford and Cambridge University players don't flock to Saracens in the way they do to more fashionable clubs. Geographically, however, Saracens are favoured, only Wasps can offer rival first-class rugby in North London.

The club is tight-knit. All officials must have played for the club and one can only vote as an ex-player. All officials live near the club, which is on the border of Middlesex and Hertfordshire, at Southgate.

England caps are rare accolades at Southgate. Sherriff was the third—all since 1945 and all forwards. John ('Ginger') Steeds, a hooker, set the trend in 1949 and 1950 with five caps in the Five Nations tournament. Next time the honour moved back a row for lock Vick Harding (a former Cambridge Blue) to win six caps in the early Sixties.

Finally, to back row and that much respected No. 8, George Sherriff. He won three caps and deserved more. He would certainly have won more if it hadn't been for the remarkable fact that he didn't start playing until he was 24. (A similar case was Peter Yarranton, Wasps and England, who did not take up rugby until he was 25.) A business colleague who was also a Saracens member persuaded George that he had the physique and strength to be a useful forward and enticed him to the club.

George had never even watched a game, apart from television, but plenty of hard physical work in the London timber and haulage trade had endowed him with muscles, and a full season in the third side transformed him into a redoubtable opponent.

When Sherriff was kept away from rugby by increasing business commitments early in the 1969–70 season, the Saracens' pack lost a lot of its fire and character. His example was needed to bring the best out of the rest.

Saracens also owe a debt to that accomplished flanker, Ian Player. He was in the England reckoning at one time and one of his proudest achievements was to build Hertfordshire into a County championship force. With a solid nucleus from his own club the County team reached the County quarter finals in 1968–69 and 1969–70. Most rugby enthusiasts agree and put it down to Saracen's influence.

In front of Sherriff and Player, John Heggadon and Brian Goodchild, once the established second row, are now, supplanted by Kevin Gaughran and Mike Smith, but the front row is subject to little alteration. John Lockwood, a robust hooker and fierce forager in the loose, has been frequently propped by Geoff Pudney and Roger Bloom.

One of the Saracens' greatest embarrassments is how to accommodate all their talented threequarters. Injury and unavailability often ease the problem as Roger Weaver will testify! Roger was elected captain in 1968–69 and promptly missed most of the season because of jaundice.

One of the most promising of Saracens' young threequarters is Hertfordshire winger Peter Cadle. He has speed, determination and a knack of scoring vital tries . . . the only thing

he lacks is a light heavyweight's physique.

In the autumn of 1970 three new arrivals added substance to the threequarter strength. Ian Vinter and David Croydon established a formidable, hard-tackling centre pairing, while Welshman Denis Stone challenged for a wing position.

Last season Ceri D'Arcy played almost throughout as Geoff Hunt's successor at full back and David Bright still proves indestructible at scrum half as Alder's partner.

Saracens' membership has soared from 200 in 1945 to 800. This allows them to run nine XV's plus a colts team every Saturday, and the coaching talents of Ken Bartlett ensure that such strength is not wasted. Did Wasps make an error in letting the former St. Luke's College flyer go to Saracens as coach when they themselves were—and still are—so urgently in need of one? Wasps' loss made the Saracens' team. But it is typical of Wasps that they have no regrets and regard it as good for the game. Ken Bartlett's teaching appointment in the vicinity of Saracens' home territory meant that he had to find a more accessible club. He remains a very welcome 'visitor' at his old club.

EXOTIC CLUBS QUIZ III

Many clubs playing in England have exotic names. Here are ten more of them, but in fact two are fictitious. Can you name these two?

1. Gloucester Old Blues 2. London Transport
3. Hawker Siddeley Dynamics 4. Diehards
5. Manchester Fire Brigade
6. Northampton Men's Own
7. Pressed Steel Fisher
8. Northampton Boy's Brigade O.B.
9. Mersey Docks and Harbour Board
10. Lockheed

Solution on Page 93

Ian Kirkpatrick, New Zealand's superb flanker

Brian Lochore, New Zealand Captain of World XV, 1971

Selecting an International Team

by Rupert Cherry

Compare your knowledge of players with that of the selectors! Rupert Cherry, a most experienced commentator watching over 100 matches each season, found he had never seen a third of the new talent which the England selectors discovered. He interviewed Albert Agar, retiring after seven years as a selector, and chairman in 1970-71.

All through the match the chap sitting next to me had been moaning about the wretched way England were playing. The forwards could not get the ball, no-one jumped in the lineout, no-one shoved in the scrum, the half-backs could not, or would not, pass the ball, if the centres got it they dropped it, the wings never saw it at all, and the full-back gave my neighbour a minor heart attack every time he touched the ball.

In the bar afterwards I heard this moaner saying "Of course, it's not the players' fault really. The selectors are to blame. They've picked the wrong men. It's always the same; been like for years. It's who's in. They've got their favourites and they pick 'em every time. They won't listen to anyone else."

Nearly everyone thinks he could pick a better team than the one that is actually chosen. Listen to the chorus in every clubhouse.

So many rugby writers feel it is their duty to name their choice that I sometimes wonder why the selectors bother at all. Why not feed all the gratuitous choices into a computer and get the right answer?

At least there would be someone else to blame when the team were beaten.

Now, I have never chosen a team in my life; not even as a schoolboy. Of course I have a fair idea of what I would do if I ever became a selector, but having endured many years of conversation on the lines I have just recounted I wondered what the actual England selectors really did. So I asked one.

I went to Albert Agar who retired from the job at the end of the 1970–71 season. I have known and talked to the last four chairmen of the England selectors about teams and players and Rugby football in general, but I had never in all those years heard from the man's own lips how he went about doing the job of selecting.

It is relevant I think to point out that the chairman is appointed for the season by the Rugby Union. He then nominates the men he would like to serve with him as the committee, and invariably the Rugby Union approve. So the chairman has the men with whom he thinks he can work best.

Agar had been a selector for seven years—that is, on the England committee. His previous experience as a selector had been with Lloyds Bank, the United Banks, and for a short time he did the job for Middlesex. He had played as a centre for Harlequins and England, but never selected for them. So he had plenty of experience of the job when the Rugby Union appointed him chairman in the 1969–70 season.

It is interesting to know what goes on in a man's mind when he first tackles the job. It so happened that Agar chose two men who had played for Northampton and England, Dickie Jeeps and Jeff Butterfield, for his committee, and later he appointed Don White, another Northampton and English International, as coach. I asked Agar if he did not feel over-loaded with Northampton men. "Speaking for myself," he said, "I forgot all about my club when I became an England selector. I think the same thing happens to other people. You tend to become national in thought. I could go to a Harlequins match, and quite honestly not care who won, although they are my own club. I would be there simply as a selector."

I suggested that he would be watching one or two or at the most three players, and he agreed. "I would not see the match, certainly not as you do, the whole thing with an impartial mind," said Agar. "I would be watching a particular man, and perhaps I would not be watching him all the time. You see he might have a reputation of being unable to last the 80 minutes. So I might decide to watch him for the last quarter of an hour. Plenty of chaps are brilliant in the first half, but of course they must be going 100 per cent at the end, too."

From the way some people talk in the clubhouse you imagine they think the selectors have no plan at all, but simply drift along to matches, meet up a fortnight before the international and then argue with each other about their favourite players. I do not suppose anyone really thinks this is what happens, but I doubt whether most people realise the tremendously complicated process of arriving at the England side.

"First of all," said Agar, "we have last season's team to go on. We know what they did, and if they failed, we know why they did so. From that we realise what needs to be done to put it right. We all realise where the weaknesses lie, and therefore know the kind of players we need to try to put them right.

"So we plan our watching. Who shall go to what matches and what kind of players we are looking for. We start off with the clubs because the counties do not get going until October, but in that month and in November we see practically every county game. Each week each selector writes a report on the players he has seen and sends this report not only to me as chairman, but to the other selectors as well."

I asked whether he arranged for selectors to watch their own kind of players, in other words did he send a former forward like Eric Evans to see forwards exclusively. "No", answered Agar, "Normally we go where it is most convenient"—remember selectors are travelling thousands of miles a season—"but if a second opinion is needed, if someone has discovered a new player, or for any reason a check is needed, then sometimes we might have a former player in his position watching him."

I do not suppose for a moment that the selection committee lacks advice and information from all sorts of people in Rugby

football, but in fact almost everything they are told is stale news. They know something about almost every player who is likely to come to the top. For one thing they keep a very close watch on the schools, and the schools' international sides. Often a youngster is marked out by the selection committee for future reference while he is still at school. When he gets into the England Under-19 side he can be sure that a selector has seen him, and his name will be noted.

"I had to wait several years for some of the players we had in 1969–70 to mature," said Agar. "When I first saw them as boys I thought they might make good. Not all of them do; but several have been worth remembering."

Next time you feel bound to utter some criticism of the England selectors just think of a comparison between their knowledge of players and yours. I, as a Press man, see perhaps 100 or more matches in a season, yet I do not get around the country like a selector. Probably a third of the new talent which the six selectors unearth between them, I have simply never seen. How very much less is the knowledge of the average member of the Rugby football public!

By the time the Divisional matches in the County Championship have been played the selectors have chosen their first trial sides. At this stage they have a fairly good idea of what the eventual side should be, or rather what they hope it will be. "We always hope the senior side in the first trial will be the England team," said Agar. "It very seldom is, because form fluctuates and people get injured, but that is always our hope."

"Perhaps that is not completely true, because sometimes, as we did last season, we

'Jacko' Page, Peter Larter and Tony Bucknall in play for England v Scotland, 1971

put a man in the junior side as a trial horse for some new player in the senior team, but leaving those adjustments aside we will by then have spent many hours discussing the players who will suit us best.

"Don't forget we are going on the principle of picking a side for a particular match. If the first game is against Wales we are picking to play Wales and we are not thinking of meeting Scotland later on. We know the kind of game we hope to play, and we know the kind of players we want to do it. We are not just picking the 15 best players in their position in the country. We have to think of how they will fit into our scheme of things, and who will make the best contribution for the team point of view. It is sometimes the case that there is a better player in a certain position, but we do not have him because he will not suit the rest of the side."

I wanted to know how the voting was managed with six members of the committee, and whether the chairman had a casting vote. Agar's reply rather surprised me. "In all the years I have been an England selector," he said, "I have never known a vote to be taken. We may discuss a player for hours, but in the end we all agree. What happens is that the selector who started with a different view from the others is finally persuaded to agree with them. You must remember," he went on, "we have agreed on the *kind* of team we want and the *kind* of game needed right at the beginning."

"And which position do you pick first?" I asked. "Well, we generally start at the top with the full-back," said Agar, "but we had no firm rule about this."

This brought an amusing story to mind that Alec Lewis, a Bath and England wing-forward in the early fifties, and now a selector, used to tell. Lewis, a great all-round sportsman, won his first cap at the age of 31; he had returned to rugby *after giving the game up for six years!* It was a tremendous achievement, but, of course, Lewis did not think of that at the time. He played in all nine times for England and was always biting his nails wondering if he had been chosen.

Years later he was talking to Carson Catcheside who had been the chairman of the selectors at the time. "There's one thing, Alec," said Catcheside, "when you were playing we never had any difficulty. We used to say, now, about the pack; first of all, we've got Lewis!"

"If only you had told *me!*", murmured Lewis.

Agar continued. "Even if the first trial goes all right, it is by no means plain sailing then. We probably spend as much time picking an unchanged side as we do making changes. We have to chew over everything. Naturally a trial is never exactly right. There is always some adjustment we have to make in one or two positions. We certainly should have the right team by the second trial, and the final should really be a practice match."

When a touring side is in Britain there are only two trials, and Agar thought that this was quite sufficient. "After all," he said. "You know what the players can do; you have seen them all several times. What you really want to see in a trial is what they can do in opposition to certain other players. From that you can gauge how they are likely to perform against the individuals from the other country whom they are likely to face."

Agar was an innovator so far as England were concerned. He started the squad system, following the Welsh example. He appointed the first official coach the England side ever had. But it was not so much due to the fact that Wales had adopted a squad

system as to Agar's own experience. He felt the need to build a TEAM, not just to select a number of individuals. He wanted to weld them together, and he wanted the right elements with which to start welding. He had learned the need for this approach under the chairmanship of "Micky" Steele-Bodger, his predecessor, whom he had served for seven years before he was appointed chairman.

I suppose in rugby history Agar's term of office will not be rated high. True there was England's victory over South Africa in 1969–70, and in the 1970–71 season the triumph of the Under-25's over the Fijians, but in the home internationals England were poor.

It was a great disappointment after such a promising beginning, and the critics fired heavily at Agar and his committee. At the end of the 1969–70 season, when the side was overwhelmed in Paris, and again in January 1971 when Wales over-ran Agar's side, it was easy to shoot him down. I believe, however, that what Agar started will come to fruition in a few years. The pity of it is that Agar could not stay long enough to gather the harvest.

EXOTIC CLUBS QUIZ IV

Many clubs playing in England have exotic names. Here are ten more of them, but in fact two are fictitious. Can you name these two?

1. Morris Motors
2. National College of Food Technology
3. May and Baker 4. Manchester Ship Canal
5. Northampton Heathens
6. Hartlepool Boy's Brigade O.B.
7. Perkins Sports 8. Aldershot Angels
9. York Railway Institute
10. Wadebridge Camels

Solution on Page 93

Rugby Boom In Manchester

by David Irvine

Tony Neary (Broughton Park and Lancashire flanker) wins a line-out for England v France, 1971

Broughton Park grow in strength and stature and their stalwart John Burgess could be the coach to revitalize the England team. Manchester have set up a £120,000 super sports-centre at Cheadle Hulme, while Sale and Wilmslow impress with their play and first-rate organisation.

There was a time, and not so very long ago at that, when no-one south of the Potteries was absolutely certain whether Broughton Park should be pronounced Brufton, Browton or Brawton. Within the relatively small and secluded pond of Northern rugby Park might well have been a moderately-sized fish; in the much larger and more competitive national lake they were still a minnow.

Nonetheless in an amateur sport where tradition, long-standing relationships and progress are rarely compatible, the apparently sudden rise to prominence of this old-established (founded 1882) Manchester club has delighted rather more people than it may have surprised.

For many decades Broughton Park were overshadowed by their two illustrious neighbours, Manchester (1860), and Sale (1861), but now the balance has at last begun to tilt in Broughton Park's favour. Certainly the bestowing of recent England honours on three forwards—Barry Jackson, Mike Leadbetter and Tony Neary—has gone a considerable way towards demonstrating to the rest of Britain that Manchester is a three-club rugby city, not two.

Although Broughton Park have played a large and significant part in the destiny of Lancashire county rugby over very many years, their real success as a club side can be traced almost entirely to their move from Eccles to their new and permanent home at Chorlton-cum-Hardy in 1955. The election of a go-getting secretary in Welshman Bill Bevan, and the shrewd appointment of the club's first official team coach, John Burgess, in 1966 really set things moving.

In 1955 Park's fixture list still reflected the somewhat parochial level at which the club functioned, the only non-Northern teams they played being Loughborough Colleges and Saracens. Today Park are prepared to travel almost anywhere for the right sort of opposition — Cheltenham, Ebbw Vale, Pontypridd, Gloucester and Bath—and welcome anyone willing to make the journey north, such as Abertillery, Saracens, Rugby, Coventry and Moseley. In Wasps' best postwar season, 1962–63, they travelled to Sudbury and beat them 14–3, one of only five defeats in the season and the heaviest.

Towards the end of the 1968–69 season, when Park opened their splendid new stand, they not only persuaded Coventry to perform the ceremony but had the considerable satisfaction of beating the Midlanders 14–12, a result which has been beyond the capabilities of most Northern clubs in recent times.

With the departure of Manchester to their luxurious and spacious new home at Grove Park, Cheadle Hulme—in Cheshire be it noted!—Broughton Park are now very much THE City of Manchester club now. Their catchment area has inevitably expanded and, although "foreigners" who move to Manchester to live, work and play still tend to make for Sale, it is to Broughton Park that the best of local talent are now attracted.

Park's policy in encouraging youngsters, reflected in the running of two Colts sides (they pioneered Colts' rugby), has paid not only regular but eventually handsome dividends. The present club captain, Mike Leadbetter (capped against France in 1970) graduated to the England side via the Park Colts, Wyverns, Griffons and first teams after making his first contact with the club at the age of 15.

If success came relatively quickly to Leadbetter and Neary—the latter, with a full international season behind him, is still only 22—then the club's first full international, Barry Jackson, found success a very different way. A stalwart of the side since the 1950s, and a man whose career has been inextricably bound into the club's changing status, Jackson re-shaped his play after years as a second-row workhorse to win England selection as a prop at a time when most men would have been prepared to call it a day.

Many clubs like to stake a claim on international players of the past through some brief or tenous link but Park, with a disarming frankness, are quite happy to admit that their first "cap" was 88 years in coming. It is worth recalling, however, that an outstanding England captain "Bert" Toft captained Park from 1932 to 1935, before moving on to similar positions with Waterloo, Lancashire and England, while Rear-Admiral S. P. Stuart, who played for England in 1907, began his career with Broughton Park. In more recent times the club has produced England trialists—from the former prop Eddie Crewe to Alan Shuker (a Barbarian and the 1970–71 Lancashire president), Ron Greenall and the present hooker Peter Barratt. For a great many years, Park has provided distinguished players to Lancashire, including *ten* on one famous occasion.

One name which is not to be found in the international, trial or Barbarian record books, however, is that of John Burgess, the man who has probably done more than anyone else to raise and revitalise the club on the actual field of play. A wing-forward of notable vigour (he played for the club until he was 40 and for N. W. Counties against the All Blacks at 39) Burgess accepted the post of club coach at the start of the 1966–67 season. He was so successful that Park had one of the finest seasons in their history, winning 34 games and losing only seven.

Two years later he graduated to a similar post with Lancashire and again made immediate impact. Lancashire won the title and very nearly repeated the performance the following season. His dedication, single-mindedness and unshakable belief in the value of coaching did not go unnoticed in higher quarters either, and he was ultimately appointed assistant manager and coach to the England side to tour the Far East in 1971. His reputation now is an international one.

In a sport where an honour of this sort is normally reserved for an ex-international, this could well be an important and highly significant breakthrough for the man who has more to offer than performance on the field of play. After all some of the finest school coaches were not outstanding players. The important point is that Burgess is out and out a players' man. The response to his often apparently excessive demands on those under his charge is an education to see, for he commands tremendous respect. Certainly it is to Burgess that Jackson, Leadbetter and Neary claim they owe their caps.

With a population of close on one million in the greater Manchester area, and in spite of the counter-attractions of world-class soccer and Rugby League, the region is quite able to sustain a number of first-class Rugby Union clubs. In the 1969–70 season Sale had one of their finest seasons ever under the captaincy of their Lancashire scrum-half Alan Morritt; Wilmslow, a little further out, have made great strides and pioneered floodlight football in the area. Manchester, if somewhat unsuccessful on the field of play, have shown commendable initiative and foresight in joining with the Cheadle Hulme cricket club in setting up a massive sports complex costing over £100,000 at Grove Park.

Although there is widespread disappointment at the decline of playing standards in the Manchester club, particularly when compared to the trend at Broughton Park, Sale and Wilmslow, members had some slight compensation last season with the selection of full-back Dr. Barry O'Driscoll for Ireland after a long and patient wait in the shadow of the great Tom Kiernan.

Nevertheless Manchester's future as a club is bright. Standards are rising in the junior teams, where there is no shortage of players, and in Grove Park they have the basis for what could well prove the beginning of a new era. Geographically it is ideally situated close to Ringway Airport and the M6; scenically it offers a delightful setting with ample room for expansion. From the point of view of facilities, there are some excellent squash and badminton courts. Sir William Ramsay visited the club during his Presidential year and was greatly impressed with what he saw there. Many people are confident that the future of the game lies in sports centres such as this.

It could be that if the RFU decide to finance regional grounds, Grove Park could be the choice in the North-west. At least this is what Manchester hopes.

Wilmslow, too, are making a considerable impression, and made a particularly good job of staging a recent England trial, while their efforts on the field seem to grow stronger every year. Indeed it is Wilmslow and New Brighton, rather than Sale and Birkenhead Park, who provide the bulk of the players to Cheshire these days,

To an older generation, Sale is still the club which symbolises rugby in the Manchester region. Their fixture list is still by far the strongest — with Northampton, Coventry, Leicester, Moseley and Bedford from the Midlands; Rosslyn Park and Wasps from London; Gloucester, Bristol and Bath from the South-west; and an attractive cross-section of the best teams in Wales, Ireland and Scotland.

Although their results in the 1970–71 season did not match their outstanding record in 1969–70, when they won the *Sunday Telegraph* pennant (Broughton Park won it three years earlier) as the outstanding club in the North, and stand-off Chris Toone scored 264 points, they are still one of the country's best-respected clubs with a high reputation for hospitality, friendship and good football.

Sale—with England wing Jim Roberts as Fixture Secretary—believe they will come again in the near future for they now possess two of the finest young prospects in the North playing in their back division—John Horton, who joined the club in March, 1971, from St. Helens, and Geoff Evans, a brilliant Coventry centre now on a three-year course at Manchester University. Both played in the same England Schools Under-19 team and both have already won county honours, Horton with Lancashire and Evans with Warwickshire.

Down through the years some of the greatest names in Rugby football have been associated with the Sale club. Claude Davey and Wilf Wooller both captained Wales as Sale members in the thirties, and Ken Fyfe was similarly honoured by Scotland. After the war two more Sale men, Joe Mycock and Eric Evans, captained England. Peter Stagg, the only international in the present side, has played 28 times for Scotland at the last count as well as being one of the club's three British Lions. "Hal" Sever and Duncan Shaw are only two more of Sale's famous players.

Northern rugby has its own distinctive flavour and for that it owes a considerable debt to clubs like Sale and Manchester for their efforts past, present and future. More recently the same has come to be said of Broughton Park and Wilmslow. To some people who read the headlines but never the small print, it may seem that soccer is the only game played in Manchester—but nothing could be further from the truth. Rugby is flourishing now as never before and the signs are that the new prosperity which the game has enjoyed in the area during the last 10 years will not only continue but increase.

RESERVE FIFTEENS

The following Ten Names are the names of the Reserve XV's of Ten Rugby Union clubs. Can you name them?

1. Druids 2. Vikings 3. Vandals
4. Scorpions 5. Wild Geese
6. United (a West Country club)
7. Wanderers (not London club)
8. Athletic (a Welsh club) 9. Heathens
10. Seahorses

Solution on Page 94

Major Moves In English Rugby

by John Reason

England's first-class clubs are moving steadily towards a Championship set-up, while English rugby seems certain to have eight new regions, with three types of club . . . senior, intermediate and junior . . . in each region.

When you consider that the Scots have had their Border League for more than seventy years and that the whole structure of French rugby is based on a league championship, it really is quite extraordinary that the Rugby Football Union should have got itself into such a tangle about the introduction of a league championship among the first-class clubs in England.

The story really began when the 1968 British Lions returned from South Africa after losing yet another series. David Brooks and Ronnie Dawson, the Lions manager and coach, felt that the biggest difference between the teams was in the strength of their will to win. Both saw this as a consequence of the lack of competition in British club football. Both thought that each of the four Home Unions should either create that competition or resign themselves to sending losing teams abroad for ever.

This struck a spark among the clubs. The fuel for the blaze had been there for years. Years of inflationary government were crippling the clubs financially and in an age when television was giving everyone a microscopic look at the grass on the other side of the fence, the clubs decided that they were providing the training ground for the players whose skills financed the whole game, and in return they were getting practically nothing.

Their season is an abortion, and always has been. By the time they develop some team skills in early autumn, the county championship arrives like a largely unwanted cuckoo to foul up the nest. It provides a host of extra games and practices which the players in more than half the country do not want but which they feel they cannot avoid if they want to be considered for the England team. The worst aspect of the intrusion is that in London and the Midlands, where the strength of English rugby lies, the county championship represents a sizeable step down from what the players achieve with their clubs, instead of a step up.

No sooner does the county championship come to an end in December than the international season starts. Clubs lose their top players to largely unnecessary trials and then lose them again to the international matches. Nine times out of ten, they also lose matches to bad weather during the months of the international season.

In fact, the club season has already been dead for weeks, but gallantly they struggle on and somehow arrive at Easter and the better weather. By then, everyone is fed up with rugby and they simply want to go off on their Easter tours, play a few games of Sevens and pack up for the summer.

When you consider that this has been the pattern of a club rugby season in England since the Lord above knows when, it astonishes me that the game has even survived. The whole structure is an anti-climax from start to finish. Indeed, it is a series of anti-climaxes. The club season never reaches a peak. It just goes downhill.

This was tolerable in an age when costs were fairly stable, but as inflation broke into a trot and then into a gallop, the clubs found themselves in the same situation as Rolls-Royce. Costs escalated and they were not getting sufficient return for their product.

This situation existed for years before David Brooks came back from South Africa. He just fired the gun which started the avalanche, so in retrospect, the only remarkable aspect of the development was that the first-class clubs had not banded together to discuss their common problems.

Anyway, that is what they did late in 1968 and the thing which surprised them all was the bond of interest which united them. They suddenly realised how little true representation they had in the governing body of Rugby football. They suddenly realised how much out of sympathy they were with the constituent bodies. Most of the first-class clubs are run by men who are truly at the heart of Rugby football in England and it suddenly struck them that the tail was wagging the

David Sellar (Loughborough Colleges) in full flight

dog and it had been doing it for so long that it was ridiculous.

The clubs also agreed that they wanted to start a league championship, but that was taken so much for granted that in a way it was almost incidental to the other bonds which they discovered were uniting them.

The clubs said that they were considering the idea of starting a regional club championship, largely from existing fixtures. The idea was to divide the country into four areas — London, the Midlands, the North and the West. These four areas would produce regional champions and runners-up from each of four leagues in which all the clubs would play each other once. In London and the Midlands, this meant seven or eight matches for each club out of a total fixture list of something like 35. Really, it was a very small proportion. In the North and the West, the clubs would have been involved in something like 12 league matches.

It was suggested that the leading clubs from each area would then go into a national knock-out from which would emerge the champion club of England.

The beauty of the idea was that it would have given the clubs a properly balanced season for the first time in their history. Instead of dying before Christmas, the club season would have built up to a peak in the Spring, just as in France and in every other spectator sport played in the winter.

Rugby football would have had its own league championship and its own Cup Final to divert some of the publicity and attention and even some of the revenue from the Football League and the F. A. Cup. March and April would have been vibrant months instead of weeks of semi-consciousness.

At that point, the Rugby Union should have tested the water. It should have set up a committee to investigate the needs of the clubs. Unfortunately, it did no such thing. Its first reaction was to throw up its hands in horror at the very idea of a league. Even worse, it got into such a state of panic that it issued one of the most ill-advised statements ever to come out of Twickenham.

The statement was bad because it left the Rugby Union with no room to manoeuvre and no way of retreating. Without testing the opinion within the game, it committed the Rugby Union to total rejection of league competition. Any politician or general worth his salt would have shut his eyes in disbelief. The statement paid no account to the fact that the international championship is a league; that the inter-Services championship is a league; that the county championship is a league; that the whole of French rugby is based on a league and that the conservative Scots had been happily playing league rugby since the last century!

The statement accepted that the clubs needed some form of competition, but said that this should be inclusive rather than exclusive, and that therefore it would be better to explore the possibilities of a knockout cup which could include every club in the land.

Instead of allowing themselves to be stampeded by two Northern representatives into issuing such a statement, it would have been much, much better if the Rugby Union had gone to the clubs and asked them what they thought.

There were two questions that should have been asked: (1) Do you object to the first-class clubs taking part in a league competition among themselves? (2) Would you like to take part in a national knock-out cup competition?

Now I have been connected with junior club administration far longer than I care to

remember, and indeed I was connected with it long before I became a journalist. I am absolutely certain that 90% of all clubs would have said "No" to the first question and that something like 65% of all clubs would have said "Yes" to the second question.

Most clubs could not care less what the first-class clubs do, as long as they are happy. Certainly, the majority of the junior clubs have much more sense than to want to play the first-class clubs.

Unfortunately, the second question was the only one that was put to the clubs, and it was conveniently assumed that the answer to it meant that the junior clubs also objected to the idea of a league among the senior clubs. This assumption was quite wrong.

The knock-out cup scheme was only ever put forward as a red herring to divert attention from the real issue, which concerned the principle of league competition.

This happened in the first few weeks of 1969, and it only increased the determination of the first-class clubs to develop their case. The chairman of the clubs' committee was Ronnie Boon, of London Welsh.

Soon after this, the Harlequins withdrew their support from the rest of the clubs who wanted to form a league. The Harlequins is the only club in England with a big representation on the Rugby Union, and conversely, the Harlequins is the only club in England upon which the Rugby Union has a significant influence! The irony of the situation was that David Brooks is a Harlequin.

Some of the London clubs, who remembered what happened to the projected London league when the Harlequins withdrew their support, wondered if their latest withdrawal would also cause the collapse of this new initiative.

Not a bit of it. The great clubs in the

Midlands raised their eyebrows and said, in effect, "We are sorry the Quins have left us, but that's their decision. We think they will regret it."

This was the turning point. I remember thinking then that by vacating the unwritten leadership of the first-class clubs, the Harlequins had taken one of the most unfortunate decisions in their history.

While this was going on, the Scottish clubs were also pressing for a league competition and the Scottish Rugby Union took good care not to make the same mistakes as the Rugby Football Union.

Their initial reaction was exactly the same as the Rugby Union's. They were agin it! But . . . they tested the water! They sent one of their most respected men across the length and breadth of the country, and he asked questions and he preached no sermons. When he got back, he presented a report which confirmed that the Scottish clubs *DID* want to take part in a league competition, and how they wanted to organise it.

The Scottish Rugby Union have always taken the view that it is their duty to serve the clubs, and to try to give them what they want. In any case, they pointed out that the existence of the Border League invalidated any more objections they might have had to the idea of a league competition. So in Scotland, league competition became not a question of if, but how, and when.

By this time, the Rugby Union were being driven into a corner. The clubs had established that leagues had always been a part of Rugby Union football. They had pointed out that the basis of club Rugby in England is that clubs play whom they want, and that the logical end of the road being pointed by the

Steve Williams (Loughborough Colleges) gets up steam!

Rugby Union was some sort of fixture control.

They had established an unanswerable case financially, so much so that the Rugby Union said rather sheepishly that it was considering financial support for clubs involved in heavy travelling expenses.

Finally, the clubs had pointed out that with costs rising as they were, the only way for them to stay in business was to take a slice of the entertainment cake which up to now has been swallowed exclusively by Association football and Rugby League.

As they said, club fixture lists had always been exclusive rather than inclusive. Indeed, if anyone was looking for a definition of the ultimate in exclusiveness, he would be pushed to find a better example than the Harlequins fixture list. Not that the other clubs complained about that. Their attitude was: Good luck to the Harlequins!

However, the Rugby Union rejected the clubs' proposals for a regional league competition, and instead proposed a knock-out cup competition aimed at involving all the clubs. Ronnie Boon said that he did not see how first-class clubs could afford to set aside four or five or even six Saturdays a year for such a completely unknown quantity as an open knock-out cup. He said:

"It would do nothing to improve the standards of the game, and indeed some of the results could be so one-sided that it would be an embarrassment to everyone. What we need is continuity of competition and interest. That is the only way standards will rise."

The Rugby Union's scheme sought to involve the majority of the first-class clubs in the last 32 of a knock-out competition. The junior clubs throughout the country would have to compete for the few remaining places.

The eight clubs in the Midlands voted first and unanimously rejected the scheme. All but one of the clubs voted against it in London with one abstention. The North voted against it unanimously. The West accepted the view of the majority.

The first-class clubs had suggested a compromise scheme. They said that if they were allowed to run their four leagues to produce eight or 16 qualifiers, they would be prepared to go into a knock-out competition against eight or 16 qualifiers from the junior clubs, providing the first round was seeded.

This seemed the best way out of the impasse, but it meant the Rugby Union accepting the principle of league competition, and they were not then prepared to do it.

The Rugby Union met again on January 22, 1971, and after a meeting in which they talked themselves dizzy all day long, they surprised everyone by announcing that they would go ahead in 1971–72 with a pilot scheme for a club knock-out championship.

In the first year, the intention was to appoint a committee to select arbitrarily 32 clubs to take part in a knock-out. That committee would then be empowered to make recommendations about the competition for subsequent years, and to suggest a scheme which would make the competition open to every club in England.

The first-class clubs were invited to nominate four delegates to serve on the 13-man committee, and they did so. The men they nominated were Tony Vyvyan (London), Jack Barker-Davies (Midlands), Jim Bryan (West) and Jim Roberts (North).

These men were nominated at a meeting of the first-class clubs late in February. That meeting was as unanimous as ever in its determination to stick to the principles of continuous competition which it sought, but it felt that the least the clubs could do was to join the Rugby Union's sub-committee to see if there was any way of bridging the gap between their position and that of the governing body.

The clubs also felt sympathy for the Rugby Union at having got themselves into a position from which it was impossible to withdraw without losing face. They knew that some of the younger members of the Rugby Union felt that ultimately the Rugby Union would have to give in and that the problem was to find a way of doing it to ease the pain.

Of course, more than the principle of league competition is now at stake. The first-class clubs want more autonomy and they believe that it is time that the whole constitution of the Rugby Union was changed.

Many of the members of the Rugby Union think the same, and a sub-committee has been formed to examine the possibilities, and to estimate the structure needed in the future.

Ironically, most of this near-revolution happened in the Centenary Year of the Rugby Football Union. No doubt the arguments will take one or two more years to resolve. I have little doubt that when they are, the first-class clubs will be playing in a championship, just like the Scots and just like the French, and that the Rugby Union will be moving towards a new and much more compact constitution comprising eight regions, with the three strata of clubs, senior, intermediate and junior, being represented as such in each region. And everyone will then live happily ever after!

Answers to Quizzes

The Wanderers Quiz: Page *27*
Edinburgh, Ilford, Public Schools, Shirley, Thanet, Berkshire, Deal and Glamorgan; Berkshire Wanderers are now Reading. Odd club out is Wolverhampton.

The Park Quiz: Page *38*
Cassiobury Park, Watford (Fullerians play in the near vicinity), and Heaton Park, Manchester.

Exotic Clubs I: Page *51*
6. Bolton Toc H 10. Choristers

Exotic Clubs II: Page *64*
6. Buile Hill All Stars 9. Skipton Tigers

Exotic Clubs III: Page *75*
4. Diehards 9. Mersey Docks and Harbour Board

Exotic Clubs IV: Page *82*
4. Manchester Ship Canal 8. Aldershot Angels

Fix the Fixtures Quiz: Page *35*
3, 4, 5, 10, 11, 13, 14, 15. Thirty teams are named; only 7 are not Rugby Union—Sheffield Wednesday, Bristol Rovers, Rochdale Hornets, Swansea City, Sutton United, Arsenal and West Bromwich Albion.

Reserve Fifteens Quiz: Page *86*
1. London Welsh 2. Richmond 3. Wasps 4. Streatham-Croydon 5. London Irish 6. Bristol 7. Northampton 8. Cardiff 9. Blackheath 10. Colwyn Bay